LEARN
WEIGHT TRAINING
IN A WEEKEND

LEARN
WEIGHT TRAINING
IN A WEEKEND

DR NICK WHITEHEAD

Photography by Philip Gatward

ALFRED A. KNOPF
New York
1992

A DORLING KINDERSLEY BOOK

This edition is a Borzoi Book published in 1992 by Alfred A. Knopf, Inc.,
by arrangement with Dorling Kindersley.

Art Editor Kevin Williams
Senior Art Editor Tina Vaughan
Project Editors Mary Lambert, Heather Dewhurst
Series Editor James Harrison
Senior Editor Sean Moore
Production Controller Meryl Silbert

Library of Congress Cataloging-in-Publication Data
Whitehead, N.J.
  Learn weight-training in a weekend / by Nick Whitehead. 1st ed.
    p. cm.
  ISBN 0-679-40953-X
  1. Weight Training. I. Title.
GV546.W54 1992
613.7'13--dc20   91-24797
                                        CIP

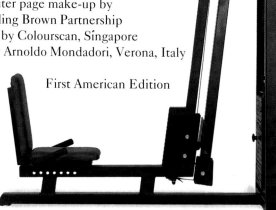

Computer page make-up by
The Cooling Brown Partnership
Reproduced by Colourscan, Singapore
Printed and bound by Arnoldo Mondadori, Verona, Italy

First American Edition

CONTENTS

Introduction 6

PREPARING FOR THE WEEKEND 8

THE WEEKEND COURSE 24

Day 1

Day 2

AFTER THE WEEKEND 84

INTRODUCTION

WELCOME TO WEIGHT TRAINING. Keeping fit by working out in the gym has now become a big part of our lives as we battle the stresses of modern living. The aim of *Learn Weight Training in a Weekend* is to teach you some basic muscle strengthening exercises in the 1½-hour workouts for each day, and to encourage you to go on and join a gym. There is no doubt that weight training can be of value to us all. It develops stamina of the heart and lungs for sports such as running; and also muscular stamina for activities such as dancing. Contrary to popular belief, no one becomes muscle-bound from weight training. As you work through the Weekend Course you will see that both men and women of all fitness levels can benefit from these exercises.

Learn Weight Training in a Weekend shows you that weight training can improve your fitness and body shape and can be an enjoyable sport in which to participate.

NICK WHITEHEAD

A HELPING HAND

Many of the **free-weight** exercises you will attempt in the gym benefit from the help of a partner. He or she can stand behind as you lie on the weight-training bench to assist you with lifting the heavy **barbell** on and off the bench **rack**, and also give you encouraging advice as you lift the weights and go through your workout.

PREPARING FOR THE WEEKEND

Getting ready mentally and physically for the course

NOW THAT YOU'VE DECIDED TO EMBARK on this weight-training project, your first step is to decide why you want to train. Do you want to lose weight? Improve your figure? Get fitter or stronger? Or train for another sport? You need to have a specific aim in mind, otherwise you will lose enthusiasm, and not make any progress. Next, you need to choose a partner. He or she will make sure you train, even when you don't feel like it, and with **free weights** they can assist and encourage you. Choose comfortable clothing and accessories to suit your budget. Before you visit a gym, try a little gentle exercise for a couple of weeks: go jogging and walking for a mile, twice a week; swim a few laps; do some stretching exercises in the bedroom; or try cycling for a couple of miles. You'll feel stiff at first but will soon feel the benefits as well. Choose a fitness center that has a well-organized, but friendly atmosphere. On your

WEIGHTS
Find out about the weights available (pp.10-13).

EXERCISE BIKE
Aerobic exercise on bikes or other machines is important to get the heart and lungs working efficiently (pp.20-21).

DUMBBELLS
Use these to improve your arm muscles (pp.10-11).

BARBELLS
Try muscle-toning exercises with this equipment (pp.12-13).

first training session make sure the instructors help you identify your weakest muscle groups, show you how to use all the weight-training equipment available in the gym and emphasize the importance of doing some **warm-up** and **cool-down** exercises. *Words in bold are given further explanation in the glossary (pp.92-93).*

HIGH-TECH MACHINES
As well as using some **free-weight** equipment, you can improve specific muscle groups, such as the legs, with the **fixed-weight machines** available (pp.16-19).

COMFY CLOTHING
Always buy clothing that is comfortable to wear. Make sure it allows you to stretch easily to all the positions necessary when doing a weight-training routine (pp.22-23).

FREE WEIGHTS

The selection that's available and what to use

THE ADAPTABILITY OF **FREE WEIGHTS** makes them ideal for home and the gym. Although initially harder to use than **fixed machines**, many exercises can be performed with **barbells** and **dumbbells**.

DUMBBELLS

Dumbbells are hand-held weights used for toning the arms. They have a short metal bar with a weight attached at each end.

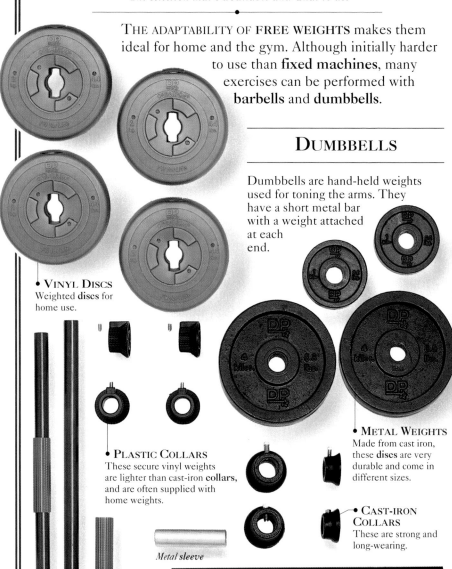

• **VINYL DISCS**
Weighted **discs** for home use.

• **METAL WEIGHTS**
Made from cast iron, these **discs** are very durable and come in different sizes.

• **PLASTIC COLLARS**
These secure vinyl weights are lighter than cast-iron **collars**, and are often supplied with home weights.

• **CAST-IRON COLLARS**
These are strong and long-wearing.

Metal sleeve

Ribbed plastic sleeve

Steel alloy bar

Steel bar

Steel bar with sleeve

Steel alloy bar with metal sleeve

ASSORTED DUMBBELLS

There are several different types of **dumbbells** available, but the same basic principle applies to all of them. Once assembled they consist of a metal bar, a **sleeve**, the chosen weights, plus the securely tightened **collars**.

Chrome executive **dumbbells** •

EXECUTIVE DUMBBELLS

These have a chrome finish, an integral textured grip, and come in either a set weight or can be adjusted to different weights. They are ideal for regular travelers.

Executive **dumbbell** *with integral textured grip* •

• *An executive* **dumbbell** *with a weight* **disc** *removed*

Executive **dumbbell** *with foam* **sleeve** •

• *An assembled, weighted, vinyl* **dumbbell**

• *A securely fixed cast-iron* **dumbbell**

ASSEMBLY INSTRUCTIONS

HOW TO ASSEMBLE

To assemble a **dumbbell** for use in weight training, hold the small bar near the floor, in case you find that the weight starts to slip. Insert the protective **sleeve** and then slide on one **collar** (A) with the wide end facing outwards; slightly tighten the screw. Slide on the appropriate weight for the exercise (B), before adding the end collar, but this time keep the wide end facing inwards (C). Always securely tighten the screws. Repeat the process at the other end.

BARBELLS

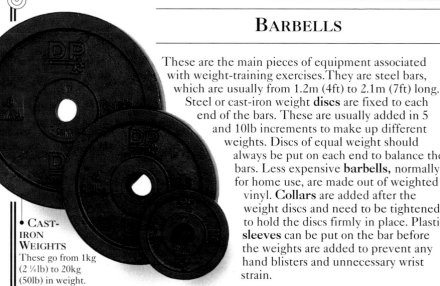

These are the main pieces of equipment associated with weight-training exercises. They are steel bars, which are usually from 1.2m (4ft) to 2.1m (7ft) long. Steel or cast-iron weight **discs** are fixed to each end of the bars. These are usually added in 5 and 10lb increments to make up different weights. Discs of equal weight should always be put on each end to balance the bars. Less expensive **barbells,** normally for home use, are made out of weighted vinyl. **Collars** are added after the weight discs and need to be tightened to hold the discs firmly in place. Plastic **sleeves** can be put on the bar before the weights are added to prevent any hand blisters and unnecessary wrist strain.

• **CAST-IRON WEIGHTS**
These go from 1kg (2 ¼lb) to 20kg (50lb) in weight.

A 1.3m (5ft) solid steel alloy bar for cast-iron discs

Chromed-steel sleeve for alloy bar

A 1.7m (5 ½ft) steel bar for weighted, vinyl discs

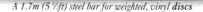

A textured plastic gripping sleeve for the steel bar

• *Plastic collars fit the solid steel bars; tighten screws with an allen wrench*

• *6.5kg (14 ¼lb) weighted, vinyl disc*

TRICEPS BAR •
This is used to develop the **triceps** muscles and also the shoulder muscles.

CAST-IRON COLLAR •
For use with **triceps** bar.

CURL BAR •
This really helps to strengthen both the **biceps** and **triceps** muscles.

• *Solid-steel curl bar for arm-curl exercises*

EASY ASSEMBLY

SECURING A BARBELL

To assemble **barbells** safely, place them on the floor or **rack**. Slip on the inside **collar** with the screw at one end (C), before you add the **sleeve**, then slightly tighten. Put on the weight **disc** (B) from the other end and add the final heavy-duty collar (A) with its secure lever tightener. Tighten both ends.

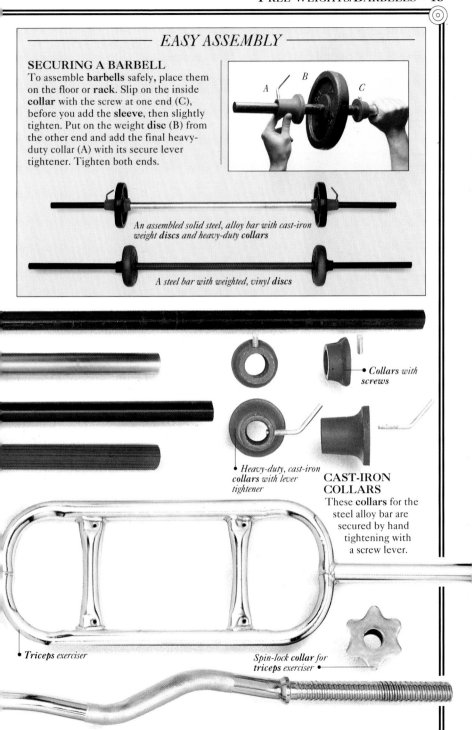

*An assembled solid steel, alloy bar with cast-iron weight **discs** and heavy-duty **collars***

*A steel bar with weighted, vinyl **discs***

Collars with screws

Heavy-duty, cast-iron collars with lever tightener

CAST-IRON COLLARS

These **collars** for the steel alloy bar are secured by hand tightening with a screw lever.

• Triceps exerciser

*Spin-lock **collar** for triceps exerciser •*

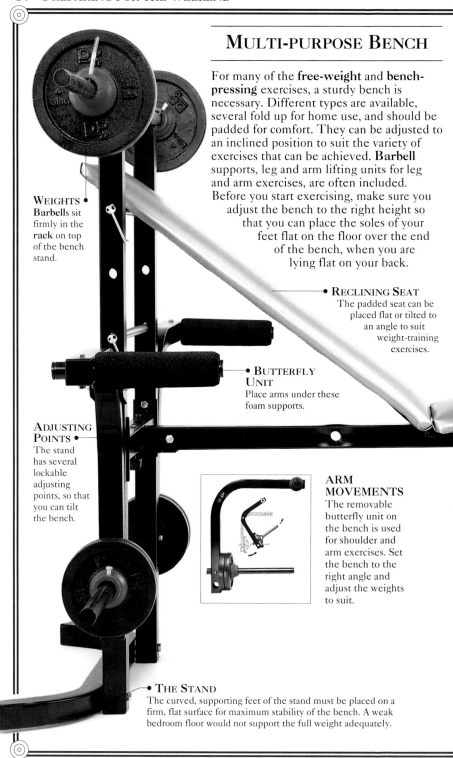

MULTI-PURPOSE BENCH

For many of the **free-weight** and **bench-pressing** exercises, a sturdy bench is necessary. Different types are available, several fold up for home use, and should be padded for comfort. They can be adjusted to an inclined position to suit the variety of exercises that can be achieved. **Barbell** supports, leg and arm lifting units for leg and arm exercises, are often included. Before you start exercising, make sure you adjust the bench to the right height so that you can place the soles of your feet flat on the floor over the end of the bench, when you are lying flat on your back.

WEIGHTS
Barbells sit firmly in the **rack** on top of the bench stand.

RECLINING SEAT
The padded seat can be placed flat or tilted to an angle to suit weight-training exercises.

BUTTERFLY UNIT
Place arms under these foam supports.

ADJUSTING POINTS
The stand has several lockable adjusting points, so that you can tilt the bench.

ARM MOVEMENTS
The removable butterfly unit on the bench is used for shoulder and arm exercises. Set the bench to the right angle and adjust the weights to suit.

THE STAND
The curved, supporting feet of the stand must be placed on a firm, flat surface for maximum stability of the bench. A weak bedroom floor would not support the full weight adequately.

ARMS
Hold the arms taut and use a partner to help you lift the **barbell** off the **rack**.

GRIP
The **barbell** needs to be grasped *outside* the **rack** uprights.

TRUNK
Your trunk must not lift from the bench during a weight-training exercise.

KNEES
As you begin to grip the **barbell** your knees should be at a 90° angle.

LEGS
Your legs help to give strong support, but always remain motionless during exercise movements.

FEET
For the best balance, firmly plant both your feet flat on the floor's surface.

LEG-LIFT UNIT
Toning **leg curl** and **leg extension** exercises (see pp.74-75) are done using this special lift attachment.

LEG WEIGHTS
Start off using low weights for your leg exercises and increase them gradually as you get fitter. Make sure the **collars** are always tight to prevent the weights from slipping.

SEAT ADJUSTER
Make sure the seat is fixed securely at a comfortable height before you start a weight-training session.

KNEE PROTECTORS
A removable foam pad to protect the knees is fixed firmly at the right height on the bench before you start a workout.

LEG MOVEMENTS
The removable leg-lift unit is a versatile bench attachment for **leg curl** and **leg extension** exercises. These help to tone up all the thigh muscles.

FIXED MACHINES

Versatile equipment to exercise the entire body

A WHOLE VARIETY OF SOLID, **fixed-weight machines**, which tone up different areas of the body, are available in modern gyms. They are easy to use on your own, and work on a weighted **pulley** system that can be adjusted to take low or high weights by just moving a fixed key bolt. Many of the exercises performed with **free weights** can be adapted to these machines. **Weight stations** are ideal for smaller gyms as they are very compact, and gym instructors can keep their eyes on several people performing different exercises at one time. Home fitness centers can be bought for home use to practice a wide range of muscle-strengthening exercises.

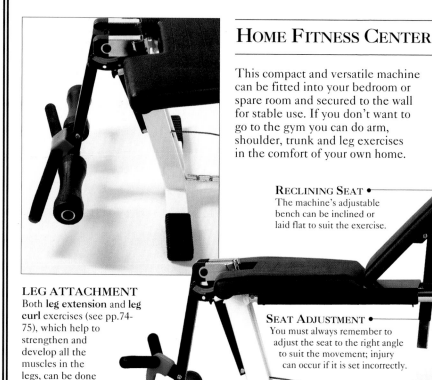

HOME FITNESS CENTER

This compact and versatile machine can be fitted into your bedroom or spare room and secured to the wall for stable use. If you don't want to go to the gym you can do arm, shoulder, trunk and leg exercises in the comfort of your own home.

RECLINING SEAT •
The machine's adjustable bench can be inclined or laid flat to suit the exercise.

LEG ATTACHMENT
Both **leg extension** and **leg curl** exercises (see pp.74-75), which help to strengthen and develop all the muscles in the legs, can be done on this versatile part of the gym.

SEAT ADJUSTMENT •
You must always remember to adjust the seat to the right angle to suit the movement; injury can occur if it is set incorrectly.

PULLEY
This **pulley** system has an **isotonic** action, which always needs some initial effort to get the weight moving.

CABLES
If the gym is used correctly, the cables remain firmly in position, but they can start to wear with constant use.

STAND
Screw the stand to a wall at the top and bottom fixings.

LAT PULL-DOWN BAR
This bar can first be used in a seated position. Pull it downwards with both hands until it rests behind the neck, to create a strengthening movement in the arms and back (see pp.66-67). If you change to a standing position, the bar can be pulled down in front of you to tone up the **triceps** muscles.

SIDE BARS
From a lying position you can push these handles up to perform a **bench press** exercise (see pp.36-37).

WEIGHT-STACKING SYSTEM
Once you've decided which weight you intend using, place the key bolt in the right hole. This will then ensure that you only lift the number of weight **discs** you desire. Push and lower the weights in a slow, controlled manner. Don't let them go halfway through an action as they will pull back down.

LEG PULLEY
Before beginning any of the leg exercises, first check that this **pulley** cable is attached to the main part of the gym.

WEIGHTS
Set the weights at a level you can easily manage and increase them gradually as your fitness improves. Don't worry if you accidentally drop the weights during an exercise, they will not injure you as they just fall back down into the **stack**.

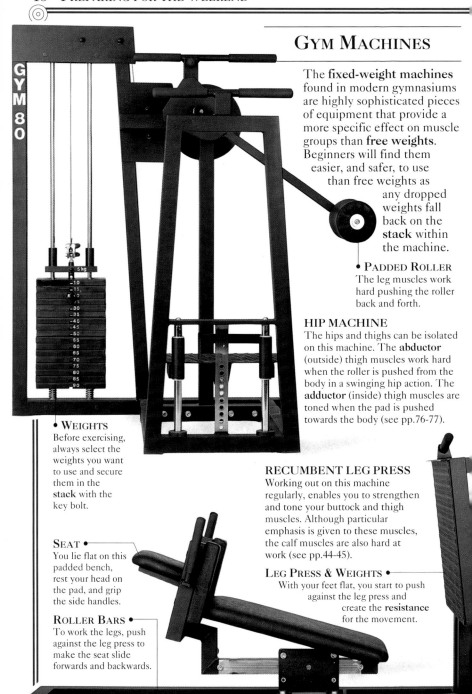

GYM 80

GYM MACHINES

The **fixed-weight machines** found in modern gymnasiums are highly sophisticated pieces of equipment that provide a more specific effect on muscle groups than **free weights**. Beginners will find them easier, and safer, to use than free weights as any dropped weights fall back on the **stack** within the machine.

• PADDED ROLLER
The leg muscles work hard pushing the roller back and forth.

HIP MACHINE
The hips and thighs can be isolated on this machine. The **abductor** (outside) thigh muscles work hard when the roller is pushed from the body in a swinging hip action. The **adductor** (inside) thigh muscles are toned when the pad is pushed towards the body (see pp.76-77).

• WEIGHTS
Before exercising, always select the weights you want to use and secure them in the **stack** with the key bolt.

RECUMBENT LEG PRESS
Working out on this machine regularly, enables you to strengthen and tone your buttock and thigh muscles. Although particular emphasis is given to these muscles, the calf muscles are also hard at work (see pp.44-45).

SEAT •
You lie flat on this padded bench, rest your head on the pad, and grip the side handles.

LEG PRESS & WEIGHTS •
With your feet flat, you start to push against the leg press and create the **resistance** for the movement.

ROLLER BARS •
To work the legs, push against the leg press to make the seat slide forwards and backwards.

ARM PADS •
Your hands grip the pads from outside, so that the forearms are pressed firmly along the length of them. By pressing hard you bring the pads inward and together.

• PULLEY SYSTEM
As pressure is put on the pads, it transfers along the **pulley** cables to raise up the chosen weights. The release of the pressure on the pads should be gradual, to keep the movement smooth.

BUTTERFLY MACHINE
This machine's movement resembles the opening and closing of a butterfly's wings. The hands grip the top of the pads and the forearms press along the sides. You then push the pads in and out. The arm and chest muscles all work hard (see pp.64-65).

• ADJUSTING SEAT
The height of the adjustable seat can be moved up and down and fixed to suit.

• FOOT REST
The angled foot rest gives a firm platform, so that the butterfly action is confined to upper arms and chest.

SEAT BACK •
A high seat back is necessary for strong support.

BACK EXTENSION BENCH
It is difficult to isolate the back muscles safely in weight-training. This **extension** bench allows the body to bend right over, at an angle, and up again to really work the back muscles (see pp.70-71).

• PADDED SUPPORT
To ensure there is no discomfort in the **abdominals** during exercising, the support is padded.

STAND •
The stand helps to hold the feet firmly.

AEROBIC MACHINES

Equipment for prolonged, energetic activity

MEDICAL RESEARCH HAS PROVED THAT by exercising at least three times a week for 15 minutes in an **aerobic** capacity, a positive improvement can be made to your level of fitness. To get the body performing aerobically, where the heart and lungs are working hard, breathing is increased, and blood circulation is stimulated, energetic exercise is needed. Cycling, rowing, and running are all ideal aerobic activities, which can now be done in the gym, or in the home, before you start your main weight-training workout.

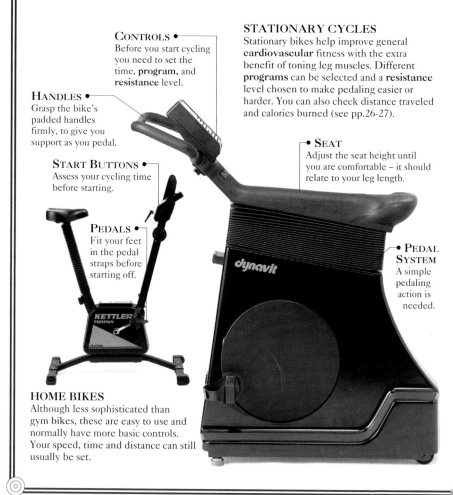

CONTROLS •
Before you start cycling you need to set the time, **program,** and **resistance** level.

HANDLES •
Grasp the bike's padded handles firmly, to give you support as you pedal.

START BUTTONS •
Assess your cycling time before starting.

PEDALS •
Fit your feet in the pedal straps before starting off.

STATIONARY CYCLES
Stationary bikes help improve general **cardiovascular** fitness with the extra benefit of toning leg muscles. Different **programs** can be selected and a **resistance** level chosen to make pedaling easier or harder. You can also check distance traveled and calories burned (see pp.26-27).

• SEAT
Adjust the seat height until you are comfortable – it should relate to your leg length.

• PEDAL SYSTEM
A simple pedaling action is needed.

HOME BIKES
Although less sophisticated than gym bikes, these are easy to use and normally have more basic controls. Your speed, time and distance can still usually be set.

STAIR MACHINE

The action of the stair machine imitates the running motion, but is a **low-impact** equivalent that works on air pressure, and causes no **stress injuries**. The pushing up-and-down movement of the legs is good **aerobic** exercise, and strengthens the **quadriceps**, **hamstring** and calf muscles of the legs. It is good preparation for active sports such as skiing (see p.81).

GRIP BAR •
The bar should be gripped with both hands to give strong support during the stepping action.

BASE •
The base is solidly built to prevent any unnecessary movement when the machine is in use.

• **CONTROL DISPLAY**
The controls on stair machines can normally be set for different times, work levels, or cadences, and strenuous **programs** such as hill training. Some machines can also indicate pulse rate and calories burned.

• **THE STRUCTURE**
The main body of the machine conceals the computerized system, which calculates the results of the various functions performed.

• **STEPS**
You stand on the steps and then push them up and down to create the necessary leg movement. For simple **aerobic** exercise, set the **resistance** to a low level; for muscular endurance, the resistance needs to be higher and is hard work.

• **PULLEY**
A simple cable **pulley** system provides the stroke **resistance** for many rowing machines.

• **HANDLE**
The handle is gripped firmly, and is pulled in and out with both hands as you row.

ROWING MACHINES

These machines provide strenuous full-body **aerobic** exercise. Many people prefer rowing to cycling, because they feel that the action provides more all-round benefit for arms, trunk, and legs. Keep a simple machine at home, or use a more sophisticated one at the gym (see pp.52-53).

• **DISPLAY**
Set the rowing time, strokes per minute, and **resistance** on the display.

• **SLIDING SEAT**
The seat slides backwards and forwards on the rails during the rowing action.

ACCESSORIES

Everything you need at the gym

WHEN YOU FIRST START WEIGHT TRAINING at the gym you do not need to impress people by going out and buying a vast selection of designer sports clothes and equipment. A small budget will buy many of the essential items from retail sports shop outlets or gym shops.

HANDY EQUIPMENT

A sports bag and sweatsuit are useful accessories right from the start of weight training; others, such as protective gloves, can be added if needed.

BAG •
A large, waterproof sports bag will carry all your gear.

• GLOVES
Fingerless gloves help protect hands when lifting weights.

• SPORTS SHOES
Gym shoes need to fit well, support the feet, and have ribbed soles for a firm grip.

BELTS •
Small, weighted belts for ankles or wrists (left) can help strengthen muscles. A waist belt (right) protects the back in heavy weight training.

• COVER-UPS
A sweatsuit helps to keep muscles warm at the start and end of a weight-training session.

GYM KIT

Choosing weight-training clothes that are comfortable to wear is more important than buying the up-to-date fashions, as so much stretching and bending is involved. Natural fabrics such as cotton, or the popular cotton-stretch fabrics, are best as they let the body breathe normally. Sweatpants, shorts with elastic waists, and all-in-one outfits like leotards, allow the weight trainer the maximum freedom of movement.

STRETCH OUTFITS
One-piece leotards are comfortable for most women to wear, but long T-shirts and shorts are equally suitable.

LEGS
Tights that stretch to fit snugly are ideal to wear with leotards, particularly during the cold months of winter.

FOOTWEAR
A wide range of gym shoes in several different styles is available for women.

SHIRTS
Loose-fitting cotton T-shirts or vests suit most men, as they do not prevent the body from sweating during **warm-up** exercises and weight training.

SHORTS
High-cut, elastic-waist shorts, or longer, stretchy cycling shorts are ideal to wear for training at the gym.

SOCKS
Padded cotton or cotton/wool socks soak up perspiration and help prevent blisters.

THE WEEKEND COURSE

Understanding the course at a glance

THE COURSE COVERS TEN SKILLS, divided into two days of practice. Starting with **Warm-Ups** (pp.26-35), you move on to weight-training for arms (pp.36-39), trunk (pp.40-43), and then legs (pp.44-47). The final skill on Day 1 is **Cool-Downs** (pp.48-51). The second day shows you more advanced weight-training exercises, building on the achievements of Day 1. Don't worry if these take longer, with practice you'll speed up.

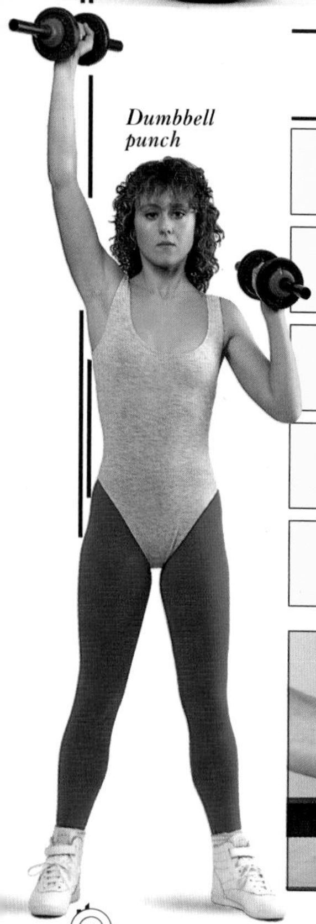

Trunk twist

Dumbbell punch

DAY 1		Minutes	Page
SKILL 1	Warm-Ups	30	26-35
SKILL 2	Arms	15	36-39
SKILL 3	Trunk	15	40-43
SKILL 4	Legs	15	44-47
SKILL 5	Cool-Downs	15	48-51

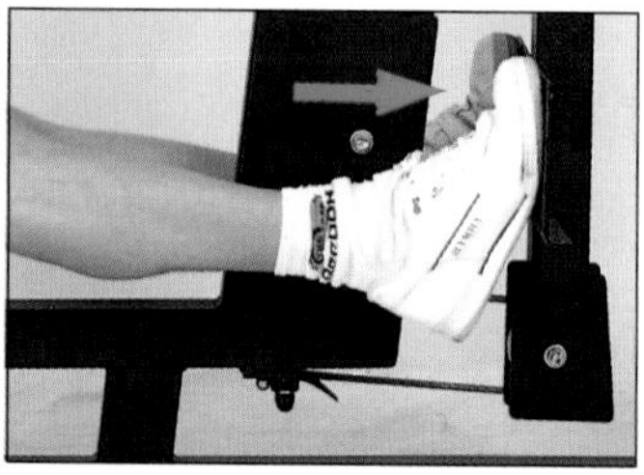

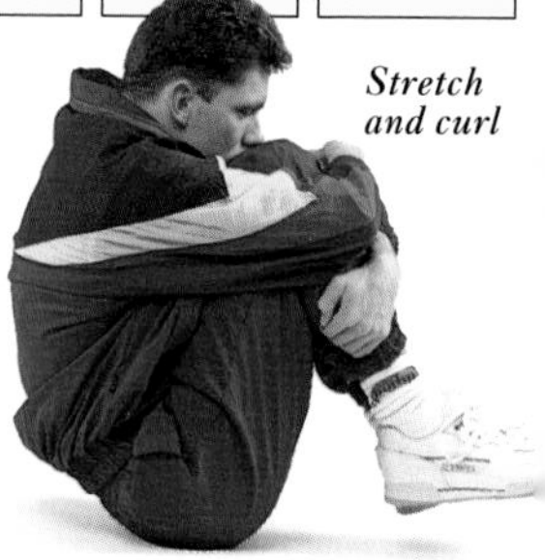

Stretch and curl

Calf press

KEY TO SYMBOLS

CLOCKS
Small clocks appear on the first page of each new skill. They highlight, through the blue colored section, how long you might want to spend on that skill, and show where the skill fits in your day. For example, look at the clock on p.36. The blue segment indicates that 15 minutes should be set aside for Skill 2: Arms, while the grey section shows that 30 minutes was spent on the previous skill. But always try and be flexible; use the clocks as guidelines only, and settle into your own natural pace.

FIGURES
The series of figures alongside each skill shows the number of steps involved for each skill. The blue colored figures help to identify the steps that are illustrated.

RATING SYSTEM •••••
Each skill is given a rating according to the degree of difficulty. One bullet (•) denotes that the skill is quite easy, while 5 bullets (•••••) show the harder, most challenging techniques.

Push-up exercise

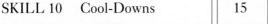

DAY 2		Minutes	Page	
SKILL 6	Warm-Ups	30	52-61	*Barbell side bends*
SKILL 7	Arms	15	62-67	
SKILL 8	Trunk	15	68-73	
SKILL 9	Legs	15	74-79	*Recumbent leg press*
SKILL 10	Cool-Downs	15	80-83	

Chest muscles

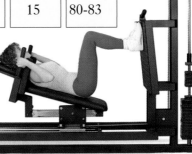

SKILL 1

WARM-UPS

Definition: *Preparing the heart and lungs for exercise*

BEFORE YOU START A WEIGHT-TRAINING session, it is important to get the heart and lungs working to their optimum level **aerobically,** and the body thoroughly warmed-up so that you don't strain any muscles. Keep your sweatsuit on initially, and do some **warm-up** exercises from the following pages to really stretch the muscles, before getting on the bike, or another of the aerobic machines.

OBJECTIVE: To get the maximum benefit from weight training.

SHOULDERS
Your shoulders are slightly dropped as for normal cycling.

CONTROLS
Remember to set the speed, time, and distance.

PEDAL POWER
The harder you pedal, the more benefit you will feel in your legs.

EXERCISE BIKES

Cycling on stationary bikes is a good **aerobic** *workout. Rating* • •

HOME BIKES

Exercise bikes are very convenient for home use. You can easily fit in 15-20 minutes of exercise every day.

— PULSE CHECKING —

FINDING THE POINT
To check whether your heart and lungs are working efficiently during **aerobic** exercise, you can take your pulse using your index fingers, and lightly press on the inner wrist or the side of the neck. Count beats for 10 seconds (first beat O) and then multiply by 6 to give your **pulse rate** per minute.
Target zone (when exercising at optimum pulse rate)

Age	Ideal rate
20-29	140-170
30-35	132-165
36-45	124-155
46-55	115-145
56-65	107-135

GYM BIKES

The bikes you find in gyms tend to be more sophisticated than home bikes. You can select different exercise **programs** and set a **resistance** level. At the end of cycling time you can normally find out how many calories you have burned off. Some bikes have handlebars that help to exercise your arms.

CONCENTRATION •
Keep checking the controls to see that you're maintaining the correct **work level**.

CONTROL PANEL •
Choose the **program** you want to do. Some are harder than others, so try them out until you find the right one.

PEDALS •
If you set a high rate of **resistance,** you'll find that you have to pedal much harder and faster to keep to the right speed.

STEADY GRIP •
Keep a strong, firm grip on the handles of the bike to give you the right support as you pedal, fast and hard, for the number of minutes you have set on the display.

• **LEG STRENGTH**
The cycling motion is a particularly good exercise to strengthen and firm up the leg muscles, especially the calves and thighs.

• **STRUCTURE**
The bikes used in gyms are very solidly made to cope with the continuous cycling. Adjust the seat height and the pedal straps before you start, so that you feel comfortable while pedaling with a smooth action.

SKI JUMPS

Warm-up aerobic exercises, which work all the body and help increase the pulse to its optimum working rate. Rating • •

ARMS •
Hold the arms right above the head, close to the ears, with hands slightly clenched. Keep looking straight ahead.

Steps 1 & 2

STRETCH AND BEND

A **ski jump** gets the heart working faster, and increases the **pulse rate**. Stand up straight with your feet apart. Stretch your arms into the air, then bend your knees and push arms forward with fists firmly clenched to resemble the start of a ski jump. Try and make all the actions one smooth movement.

• **REACH**
The most comfortable position before driving the arms back, is with your clenched fists facing inwards, and the elbows slightly bent, outwards.

• **TRUNK**
As the arms push down, your trunk is straight, due to bending the knees and hips.

LEGS •
The legs are straight and firm, but do not remain **locked** in this starting position. They do not start to tense until the arms begin the forward drive movement.

• **BALANCE**
Make sure your knees are fully bent, to make the exercise easier to perform, and to give your body the strong support it needs. Good balance is essential in this movement.

FEET •
Your feet remain rooted to the spot throughout the exercise, although you might be lifted onto your toes by sheer momentum right at the end.

Steps 3-5

FOLLOW THROUGH

Keep the momentum going by swinging your arms behind you, holding them close to the body and reach further forward, bending more as you go. Pause only briefly before driving your arms out in front again and then push upwards, stretching right up with as much strength as you can manage to really work the whole body. Maintain a steady rhythm of down-and-back, forwards-and-up. Try and remember that the **warm-up** exercises are designed to stretch the muscles and ease you gently into your day's training **program**. Repeat the exercise 3 times.

FULL EXTENT •
Once your arms reach right up to this high point, they then start the repeat of the movement by immediately driving downwards again.

EYES STRAIGHT •
Throughout all the different stages of the movement your head should be held upright, with your eyes fixed straight ahead.

SHOULDERS •
In this part of the movement your shoulders direct the arm effort upwards.

SUPPLE SWING •
Your arms may swing further back than shown here, dependent on how supple you are.

• THIGH SUPPORT
The **quadriceps** muscles play an important part in driving the body in many movements, and in several sports, such as sprinting.

FOOT HOLD •
The force of the push upwards at this phase could lift you onto your tiptoes, but do not try and hold this position for long.

ARM ROTATION

Both the arms and shoulders loosen up and become much more supple with this type of exercise. Rating ● ● ●

Steps 1-3

REACH AND STRETCH

 To warm up the arms, stand up straight with shoulders firmly back. Place arms on your legs and then space feet slightly apart. Reach out in front with your arms keeping them parallel to the feet, and then stretch right up above your head, reaching up onto tiptoes.

• EXTEND
Stretch arms as high as possible, keeping them close to your head.

• HEAD SENSE
Before you start, concentrate on breathing slowly, and evenly.

• POISED
Slowly straighten and stiffen your arms, then stretch them full out, keeping the fists clenched.

• HANDS
Relax your body and let your hands rest loosely on your thighs.

STANCE •
Plant feet on the ground, a shoulder's width apart.

TRUNK ROTATION

REACH OUT

This is a variant exercise, which is good for toning men's chests and stomachs. Start with feet apart, lean forward and clasp your hands in front (A), then push them right out. Swing your arms out to the side (B) and upwards (C), keeping your hands away from your body. Lower them back down again, before exercising in the opposite direction (D). Repeat 4 times.

Keep your eyes fixed on your hands.

Stretch sideways, keeping your balance.

A   B

Lean as far back as possible from the waist (C), before going back to the start position, and working the other side (D).

C   D

ARMS •
Press your arms backwards and downwards as far as possible.

——— Step 4 ———

SWING OUT

Extend arms wide, and then lower them back down to the side of the body to complete the exercise. This windmill action should be carried out rhythmically without stopping. The aim is to take your arms high and back, stretching all parts of your body. If your shoulders feel stiff at first, don't give up, this will soon start to ease. Repeat the exercise 4 times.

FEET •
As your arms come down, the body weight transfers back onto the balls of the feet.

• **EXERTION**
With this much stretching you are bound to feel a little discomfort in the ribs in the next few days, as you are opening up the rib cage area much more than usual. It is not harmful, and when you train regularly the ache will disappear

• **LEGS**
Don't forget to push upwards with your legs as you reach up and out. If you just confine the exercise to arm swinging, you lessen the benefits of the exercise for the whole body.

PUSH-UPS

Push-ups *are very beneficial for arms and shoulders, but when done*
well, they also work the stomach, back, and legs. Rating ••••

———————— Steps 1 & 2 ————————
HOLD STEADY AND LOWER

Position yourself on a mat on the floor
so that you are facing the ground, and
support your body weight with your hands placed flat on
the floor in front of you, and your arms outstretched. Keep
your body taut and in a straight line, resting the balls of your
feet on the ground. Gradually lower your body to the floor,
bending only your arms, until your chest touches the
ground. Concentrate on inhaling evenly through
your mouth all the time, then push up hard on
your arms again and exhale. Repeat the
exercise 4 times.

BACK •
Make sure your
back is kept very
straight during the
push-up; try not
to let it arch in the
middle or sag at all.

• **LEGS**
Keep your legs **locked** at the
knees throughout the exercise.

• **FEET**
Place your feet together, resting
the balls of the feet on the floor,
and keep them in the same spot
throughout the movements.

FLOOR CONTACT •
Lower your body slowly until your
chest just touches the floor, before
raising it again to complete the
push-up action.

FIRM POSITION •
Hold your legs steady, while lowering your
body. Try to resist the temptation to bring
them up in the air to aid the exercise.

MODIFIED PUSH-UPS

ARM STRETCH

This exercise requires less arm strength than normal **push-ups**, and can be easier to perform for women and not so strong men alike. For those unused to exercise, modified push-ups can provide a gentle introduction, from which you can progress to the more strenuous variety. Inhale through your mouth while lowering your chest to the floor, and exhale while raising your body. Repeat the exercise 4 times.

STARTING POSITION

Kneel on the floor with your arms straight, your hands flat on the ground, and your legs together. Make sure your back is completely straight, and hold your head up.

Eyes look straight ahead.

Legs are held at a slight angle to the body.

HEAD
Hold your head in natural alignment with your body to facilitate easy breathing.

Elbows are neatly tucked in.

LOWER AND PUSH UP

Lower your body, bending only your arms, until your chest just touches the floor. Push up with your arms until your body is in the kneeling position again.

ARMS AND HANDS
Hold your arms out straight, and place your hands flat on the floor, with your fingers outstretched and pointing forwards.

ELBOWS
Tuck your elbows neatly into your sides, while pushing up vigorously with your arms to raise your body.

REGULAR BREATHING
Keep breathing evenly to ensure that you move rhythmically, and do not need to rest after each step.

SKILL
1

MODIFIED CLEAN AND JERK

*After a few lifts, you will appreciate the body stretch of this action.
Rating •••*

BACK
The back muscles tighten to help take the strain of lifting the **barbell**.

KNEES •
The knees are bent and the back is kept in a straight line.

ARMS
Make sure you keep the arms straight and taut, before you start the lift.

GRIP •
Your hands firmly grip the **barbell** just outside your feet.

HOLD •
When the **barbell** is **clean lifted** to the chest, your elbows are thrust forward.

—— Steps 1 & 3 ——
CROUCH AND LIFT

Start off with a light weight, only about 9kg (20lb) is needed to get the maximum benefit from this all-body exercise, which teaches you many of the safety factors of weight training. Crouch down, feet apart, and then lean forward to grasp the **barbell** firmly. Bring it right up to the knees, keeping them bent, and the arms very taut. Hold for a moment, breathing slowly and deeply, and then **clean lift** to the chest, keeping the barbell rock steady at shoulder level.

FEET •
Your feet should be flat on the floor, pointing forwards to give full support.

ARM POWER
When the **barbell** is fully extended above your head, your arms will be completely straight and **locked.**

FULL STRETCH
The **barbell** must be firmly gripped, close to the weights and the **collars.**

Step 4
LIFT UP

Take a deep breath and **press** the **barbell** above your head in a smooth **jerk**. Take care returning the weight to the floor. First, lower it to your chest, by bending the arms, but leaving trunk and legs **locked**. Bend your knees and back carefully, as you slowly place the barbell back down on the floor. Attempt the exercise 4 times.

TRUNK
Concentrate hard on keeping your trunk firm, and straight, for maximum support of the weight. Do not lean backwards or forwards, as you are in danger of losing your balance, and possibly the **barbell.**

LEGS
Hold your legs steady with both the knees **locked.** Only begin to bend your knees again when you start to put the **barbell** down on the floor again.

SURE HOLD
Resist any temptation to raise your heels as you lift. Your feet must be firmly planted, flat on the floor.

SKILL

2

ARMS

Definition: *A series of movements involving the upper body*

NOW THAT YOU ARE THOROUGHLY warmed up, you can attempt some gentle arm, shoulder, and chest-toning exercises, to improve the **triceps**, **deltoid**, and **pectoral** muscles.

OBJECTIVE: To strengthen arm and shoulder muscles using **fixed-weight machines** and **free weights**.

BENCH PRESSING

In this exercise you push upwards against a resistant bar. Rating • •

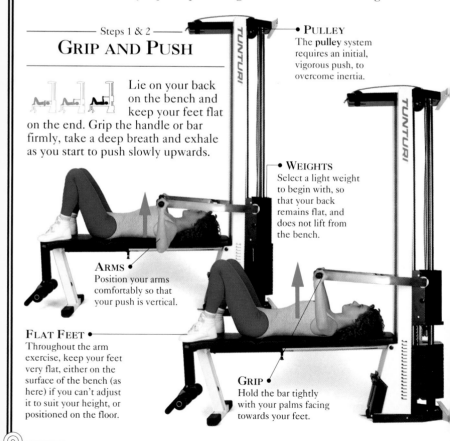

——— Steps 1 & 2 ———
GRIP AND PUSH

Lie on your back on the bench and keep your feet flat on the end. Grip the handle or bar firmly, take a deep breath and exhale as you start to push slowly upwards.

• PULLEY
The **pulley** system requires an initial, vigorous push, to overcome inertia.

• WEIGHTS
Select a light weight to begin with, so that your back remains flat, and does not lift from the bench.

ARMS •
Position your arms comfortably so that your push is vertical.

FLAT FEET •
Throughout the arm exercise, keep your feet very flat, either on the surface of the bench (as here) if you can't adjust it to suit your height, or positioned on the floor.

GRIP •
Hold the bar tightly with your palms facing towards your feet.

FREE WEIGHTS
Fix the weight **discs** while the **barbell** is on the **rack**. Lie on the bench, keeping your feet flat on the floor. Lift the barbell up until your arms are straight, and then bring it down until it touches your chest. Repeat 4 times. Your partner should stand behind you, ready to take the weight if you have any problems.

CONTROLLED RHYTHM •
The **pulley** of the **bench press** enables the bar to be moved with controlled rhythm. Do not try to force the bar up and down; this does not mean you are working harder.

Step 3
LOWER AND PUMP

Push the bar right up until your arms are straight, then pause briefly and breathe in quickly. Then lower the bar in a controlled manner to its lowest position; do not drop it suddenly. Keep the pumping movements smooth and fluid. Repeat the exercise 4 times.

WEIGHTS •
Start by using some light weights, and gradually add more until you reach an amount that you can easily lift. If you adjust the machine to a heavy weight, the exercise machine will prevent you from being injured. Do not assume you can use the same weight with a **free-weight** exercise.

• FEET
Press down hard with your feet to give you extra grip, and support, as you push the bar up and down.

• ARMS STRETCHED
The bar reaches its highest position when your arms are stretched out straight, well above your head.

MILITARY PRESS

*This exercise consists of a series of **press** movements using a weighted*
***barbell,** which tones the muscles of your chest. Rating* • • •

=========== Steps 2 & 3 ===========
HOLD AND LIFT

Breathe in and lift the **barbell**
up to your shoulders, then hold it
there, while slowly breathing out.
Then lift it right above your head, until your arms are
straight, and hold this position for a few seconds.
Keep still with your feet slightly apart.

• FULL STRETCH
Lift the **barbell** above
your head, until your arms
are straight. When fatigue
starts to set in, you will be
unable to do this.

FIRM GRIP •
Grip the **barbell** firmly with both
hands during all the lifting actions.

• MUSCLES
In this phase
of the exercise,
your arm,
shoulder, and
chest muscles
are all being
strengthened
and toned.

**TUCKED
ELBOWS •**
Keep your
elbows tucked
in, close to your
chest, and your
palms facing
uppermost.

**LOCKED
STANCE •**
Keep your legs
firmly **locked**,
while the **barbell**
is held above
your waist.

LEGS •
Make sure your legs
are slightly apart as
you straighten them
to lift the **barbell**.

• FEET
For the best
support, keep
your feet a
shoulder's
width apart,
with your toes
pointing
forwards.

ARMS
Bend your arms at the elbows, at an angle of 90°.

FEET
Keep your feet flat on the ground; it is all too easy to push them upwards during the **press** movement.

Step 4

LOWER AND RAISE

Lower the **barbell** to your chest, then lift it right up again until your arms are straight. Repeat this action 4 times. This is called the **pressing** action as you are pushing the bar upwards, and putting pressure on arms and chest. At the end of the exercise, lower the barbell slowly back down to the floor.

— MUSCLE TONING —

The muscles strengthened most during the **military press** are the **deltoids**, the **triceps**, and the **pectorals**.

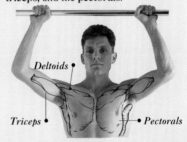

Deltoids

Triceps •

• *Pectorals*

DUMBBELL PUNCH

RHYTHMIC PUNCHING
This exercise is a gentler alternative to the **military press**. Stand with your feet slightly apart. With arms bent, hold a lightweight **dumbbell** in each hand at shoulder height. Punch the dumbbell in your right hand up into the air from the shoulders (A). Then bring your hand down to shoulder height again (B) and repeat the punching movement with your left hand (C). Breathe evenly in time to the punching of the dumbbell; as the dumbbell goes up, inhale, and exhale as you bring it down again. Repeat the exercise 4 times.

A

B

C

SKILL

3

TRUNK

Definition: *Movements to exercise the stomach muscles*

MANY PEOPLE FIND **ABDOMINAL** exercises difficult, but these strengthening exercises can be attempted by everyone. After a few practice sessions, you will find exercises appropriate to your fitness, and soon you will progress to more difficult toning exercises.

OBJECTIVE: To improve the strength of the **abdominal** muscles.

SIT-UPS

These are extremely effective exercises for toning up flabby stomach muscles.
Rating ● ● ●

——— Steps 1 & 2 ———
PREPARE AND LIFT

Lie flat on the floor, ideally on a padded mat, with your legs bent, and raise your arms to your head. Then, keeping your legs and feet still, lift your head and shoulders off the ground and reach towards your knees with your head. Hold this position for 4 seconds before lowering your shoulders again. Repeat 4 times. To vary the exercise, try touching your knees with your elbows after raising your head and shoulders.

• HEAD
Lift your head off the floor, so that you can look towards your knees.

PALM POSITION •
Keep your hands off the ground and level with your head, with the palms facing upwards.

SLIDING HANDS SIT-UPS

REACH AND PULL
This is a variation of the usual exercise. Lie flat on the floor and place your palms on your thighs (A). Then, as you raise your head and shoulders, slide your hands up towards your knees until your fingers just touch your knee caps (B).

Fingers touch knee caps

Legs bent and still

B

Hands slide up thighs

A

Feet must remain flat on the floor

• STOMACH
As you hold this position you will feel a lot of tension in your stomach muscles; this is helping to strengthen them and actually does you more good!

• LEGS AND FEET
Keep your legs bent and your feet flat on the floor during the entire movement. Concentrate hard on holding your feet in this position, so that the **sit-up** creates the most pressure in the area of the **abdominal** muscles.

• FEET
Place your feet flat on the floor, spaced slightly apart from each other. To begin with, you may find it easier to have a partner holding them firmly in the right position for you.

• EXERCISE RHYTHM
For this exercise to have the greatest effect on your **abdominals,** the rhythm should be steady: raise your head and shoulders, count to 4, then slowly lower your body down again.

TRUNK TWISTS

*The forward movement by the arms, and the twisting of the trunk,
really helps to tighten up flabby stomach muscles. Rating • • •*

——— Steps 1-2 ———
LIE BACK AND PULL UP

If you can, use a partner in this exercise to secure your feet, or alternatively press your toes under a solid object. First exercise without a weight until you get more experienced. Lie on the floor on a mat, with hands behind your head, then raise the body and twist it to try and touch your left knee with your right elbow.

—ABDOMINAL MUSCLES—

In addition to the vertical muscles *(Rectus abdominis)*, the external, **oblique abdominal** muscles are also brought into play in a **trunk twist**. Leg and groin muscles are also worked.

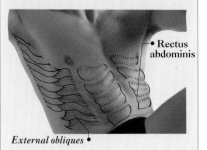

• **Rectus abdominis**

External obliques •

ELBOWS •
As you make the twist up-and-round action, point your elbows outwards to propel you round, and help increase the force of the acute sideways movement.

• **HEAD**
Your hands (with or without the weight) need to be clasped behind your head. Pull it forward in an upward movement and turn sideways for your elbow to touch your knee.

BENT BACK •
Bend your back as you come up, otherwise the groin muscles take the brunt of the strain.

LEGS •
By bending your knees and trying not to lift your feet, your legs are also being toned.

ARMS AND SHOULDERS
Although this is primarily an **abdominal** exercise, the tension created in the arms and shoulders helps to strengthen them.

LEG POWER
The strongest effort exerted by the legs is usually on the upward movement, where they help support the action of the whole body.

BACK TWIST
The *Latissimus dorsi* get plenty of exercise in the upward movements of the **trunk twist**. Keep your knees reasonably close together to avoid any strain on the groin.

FIRM STOMACH
Building up the strength of the trunk and stomach is very important as this is the main area that can easily turn to flab.

FEET
This exercise is easier to do if you **anchor** your feet firmly beneath a solid object. Try pulling up without securing your toes and you will notice how much more difficult it is!

Steps 3-4

TWIST AND TOUCH

You complete the action by getting as close to the left knee with your right elbow as you can. Then lower yourself back down to the floor again, before pulling up and working the other side, reaching for the right knee with the left elbow. Once you feel you have mastered a very rhythmic movement, try doing the exercise with a light weight to make it more difficult. For all stomach exercises make sure you exhale on the way up, and inhale on the way down. Attempt the exercise 4 times.

SKILL

DAY 1

4 LEGS

Definition: *Series of movements to exercise the leg muscles*

EXERCISES TO STRENGTHEN YOUR LEGS need to be selected carefully to ensure you obtain the desired effects. The specific movements demonstrated in this skill use both gym machinery and **free weights** to help you tone your leg muscles.

OBJECTIVE: To improve the strength of the thigh and calf muscles.

RECUMBENT LEG PRESS

This machine is specially designed to shape and tone the leg muscles, particularly the thighs. Rating • • •

LEG POSITION •
Bend your legs at an angle of 90°, and then place both your feet flat against the plate of the leg **press**.

BACK •
Keep your back flat against the padded bench of the **press**.

Step 1

PREPARE AND PUSH

Lie down on the machine. Grip the handles, fixed each side of the head rest, and place your feet against the leg **press** plate. Push against this until your legs straighten. This will raise the weights and push the seat backwards.

HEAD •
Rest your head against the pad during the exercise, breathing steadily all the time.

CALF MACHINE

STRETCH AND PUSH

The calf muscles of the leg are often neglected. One way to ensure they are kept in trim is to follow this exercise. Sit at the machine with your back straight and your legs stretched out in front of you. Hold the handles while you push with your feet against the machine's backplate. Although your whole body tenses with the effort, the calf muscles are the ones that are used the most.

— Step 2 —

BEND IN AND OUT

Slowly bend your legs again. This will cause the machine's seat to slide forwards and make the weights descend. Then stretch your legs again, and repeat the movement 4 times to develop your thighs and calves.

FEET •
Although the effort is made through your feet, this results in the thigh muscles being strengthened.

• LEGS
Keep legs apart, and your feet parallel. Push until your legs straighten before starting again.

• PULLEY
This leg machine works by the use of the **pulley** system, enabling you to move the weights up and down, even though your feet move only a short distance.

• USING WEIGHTS
Select the number of weights you wish to lift here, and fix them in place with the key bolt. It is best to start with a small number at first, slowly adding more until you reach an attainable level.

• SPARE WEIGHTS
As you become more adept at this exercise and your leg muscles become stronger, add more weights from this **stack**.

SKILL 4

HALF SQUAT

*The **half squat** helps improve the hips and thighs. Rating ••••*

———— Steps 1 & 2 ————
HOLD AND BEND

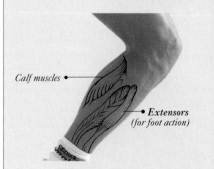

The **half squat** is an equally good exercise for men and women to practice. It needs to be performed carefully, so it is useful to have a partner to help you. With the aid of your partner, place the **barbell** with a low weight on your shoulders. Roll a towel around the metal bar if your shoulders are sensitive. To give more support to your feet, balance on some weight **discs**. Keeping your back straight and head upright, firmly hold the barbell on your shoulders and bend your knees before pushing back upwards to the start position. Attempt the exercise 4 times.

RAISED STANCE •
To prevent possible injury to your **Achilles** tendons, raise your heels by standing on weight **discs**, or use small blocks of wood. Place your feet a shoulder's width apart.

KNEES •
Bend your knees, while pushing forward with your thighs and balancing on your toes.

———— *LEG MUSCLES* ————

The strong bending action of the knees in the **half-squat** movement helps to tone up and increase the suppleness of the leg muscles. Particular emphasis is given to the development of the calf, knee, **extensor**, and thigh muscles.

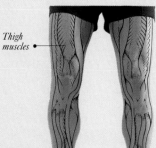

Calf muscles •

• *Extensors (for foot action)*

Thigh muscles •

• SHOULDER LIFT
Once you've lifted the **barbell** onto your shoulders, keep it horizontal and in place at the back of the neck.

— *HELPFUL HINTS* —

HANDLING FREE WEIGHTS
Lifting **barbells** is more skilful than working out on the **fixed-weight machines,** so it's worth following a few hints before attempting the **half squat.**
• Wear a weight belt (see p.22) to support the lower back muscles.
• Make sure your heels are off the floor during the exercise.
• Keep toes and knees pointing forwards at all times.
• Try to have a partner standing by at all times to assist you.

• LEGS
As you grip the **barbell** on your shoulders you will feel the tension increase in your thighs.

• EYES FRONT
Keep your head up, and fix your eyes halfway up the opposite wall.

GRIP •
Grip the **barbell** near to its **collars,** balancing it on your shoulders, as you make the **half-squat** movement.

BACK POSTURE •
Keep your back straight and concentrate hard on a sitting-down motion as you begin to bend your knees.

THIGHS •
Holding the **barbell** can make your thighs start to shake. Concentrate on keeping them above the feet, and don't let them go further apart.

FEET •
The strong upward movement starts at the feet, but they do not lift off the floor or the weights.

• ARMS & SHOULDERS
Although primarily a leg exercise, your arms and shoulders get strengthened by receiving the **barbell,** gripping it, and unloading it on the **rack** afterwards.

• CALVES
Although the heels are raised up for support, you will still find that some pressure is exerted on the calf muscles.

5 COOL-DOWNS

Definition: *Exercises performed after a weight-training session*

IMMEDIATELY AFTER COMPLETING YOUR weight-training session, you must put your sweatsuit back on to prevent the muscles getting cold. You can then start the gentle exercises that help return your body to its normal state.

OBJECTIVE: To return the body to a relaxed state while removing waste products from the muscles.

STRETCH & CURL

*The slow action of the **stretch and curl** helps reduce muscle tension. Rating • •*

——— Steps 1 & 2 ———
REACH OUT AND UP

Start the exercise by lying flat on your back on a mat on the floor, with your arms reaching out behind your head. The rest of your body is relaxed and fully stretched out from your rib cage, right through to your toes. You then slowly raise your arms and trunk, feeling the strong pull in your lower back, and start to lift yourself up, bending your knees and dragging your heels firmly towards your buttocks.

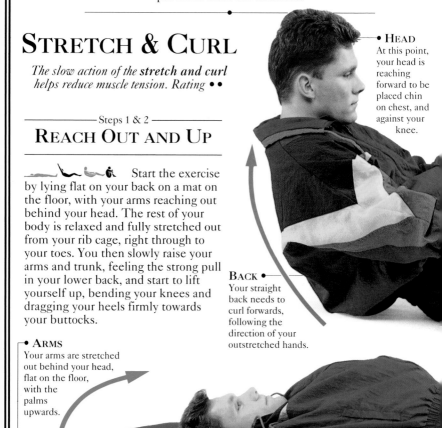

• **HEAD**
At this point, your head is reaching forward to be placed chin on chest, and against your knee.

BACK •
Your straight back needs to curl forwards, following the direction of your outstretched hands.

• **ARMS**
Your arms are stretched out behind your head, flat on the floor, with the palms upwards.

Step 3
CROUCH AND TENSE

In this final phase of the exercise, you make yourself as small as a ball as you sit right up and grasp your knees. Hold for about 4 seconds before slowly lowering yourself down again. Attempt the exercise 4 times.

HEAD SUPPORT
With the force of the movement, your head will be pushed right forward between your arms and close to your knees.

ROUNDED POSTURE
As you clutch your shins in the curl position, your back is fully rounded.

HANDS
Your arms cross over the legs, and your hands grasp each opposite shin tightly.

LEGS
Keep your legs fully bent in the curl position, and try to get them tucked well in.

LEG BENDS
When bending your legs, do so slowly to provide a good contrast between tension and relaxation.

STOMACH
As you lie flat out, your stomach muscles are fully stretched.

FEET
In the start position, point your toes upwards ready for the stretch action.

BREATHING

This exercise shows you how to control your rate of breathing after a weight-training session. Rating •

DEEP BREATHING

Lie down on your back with your legs apart and bent at the knees with the soles of your feet flat on the floor. Your arms lie loosely by your side, so that your whole body is very relaxed. Breathe in slowly and deeply through your nose, filling your lungs; hold for 2 or 3 seconds, then exhale slowly. Repeat this exercise 4 times, and try to concentrate on each breath.

• CHEST
As you breathe in deeply, you will feel your chest rise as your lungs fill with air. As you exhale, your chest moves down again, as your lungs expel the air. By breathing slowly and deeply, you will be using all the muscles of your chest and **abdominal** area fully.

• RELAXED LEGS
Bend your legs at the knees and keep the soles of your feet flat on the floor.

• ARMS
Place arms by your side to assist your breathing rhythm.

COOLING DOWN

THE BENEFITS
After a weight-training session, it is advisable to carry out a few **"cool-down"** exercises wearing a sweatsuit, before you leave the gym. These can be beneficial in several ways:
• They allow your breathing rate to return to normal, slowly.
• They reduce your body's **pulse rate**.
• They assist in the dispersal of waste products from your muscles.
• They help your body to adjust from aggressive exercise to a calmer state.
• They relax you, reducing body tension.

EXERCISES
Here are some other simple cool-down exercises for you to try out and give some added variety to your exercise routine:

• JUMPING JACK – Stand with your legs together and your hands at your sides. Jump in the air, and clap your hands above your head. Land with your feet apart. Then jump up and clap again, landing with your feet together. Repeat 5 times.

• KNEE PRESS – Lie on your back and bend your left knee. Grasp it with your hands then pull it slowly towards your chest. Press it back again. Change to your right knee. Repeat 5 times.

• ALTERNATE TOE TOUCH –
Stand with your feet apart and hands on your hips. Bend knees and touch left toes with right hand, then stand up straight again. Change to touching right toes with left hand. Repeat 5 times.

JOGGING

*This **cool-down** exercise involves running slowly on the spot while shaking your body. Rating •*

• HEAD MOVEMENT
Continually move your head and neck gently up and down, and round and round in circles while jogging on the spot.

• SHOULDERS
Shake your shoulders loosely, keeping your arms down by your sides.

HAND SHAKE •
Shake your hands and wrists in a floppy manner.

• ON THE SPOT
During this jogging exercise, stay in one spot, making sure your feet barely leave the ground.

• LEGS
Shake your legs, as you lift each foot off the ground, to loosen up all your leg muscles.

RUN AND SHAKE

Jog slowly on the spot, gently shaking all parts of your body as you do so: move your head up and down and in a circular fashion, shrug your shoulders up and down, shake your wrists so they feel floppy, and shake your legs as you jog. Continue for 1 minute. This **cool-down** exercise relaxes your muscles, and is appropriate for everybody as it relieves all pent-up tension. Attempt the exercise 4 times.

SKILL

WARM-UPS

Definition: *Gentle movements to warm up the body muscles*

THESE **WARM-UP** EXERCISES DIFFER from those on Day 1 (see pp.26-35) to add variety to your exercise schedule. However, their function is exactly the same – to warm up your muscles in readiness for a full weight-training session.

OBJECTIVE: To enable you to avoid muscle injury and gain maximum benefit from the workout.

ROWING

*A fast **aerobic** exercise that warms up all your body muscles in readiness for other exercises. Rating* • • •

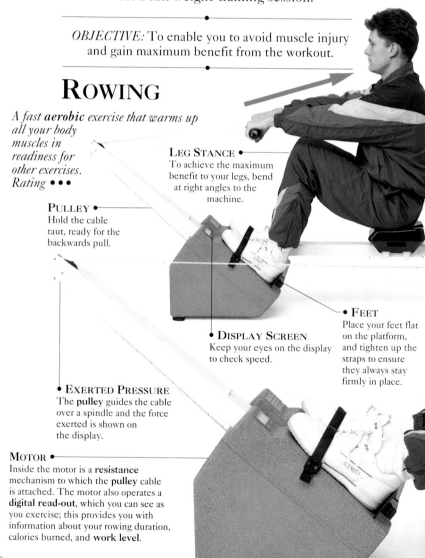

LEG STANCE •
To achieve the maximum benefit to your legs, bend at right angles to the machine.

PULLEY •
Hold the cable taut, ready for the backwards pull.

• FEET
Place your feet flat on the platform, and tighten up the straps to ensure they always stay firmly in place.

• DISPLAY SCREEN
Keep your eyes on the display to check speed.

• EXERTED PRESSURE
The **pulley** guides the cable over a spindle and the force exerted is shown on the display.

MOTOR •
Inside the motor is a **resistance** mechanism to which the **pulley** cable is attached. The motor also operates a **digital read-out**, which you can see as you exercise; this provides you with information about your rowing duration, calories burned, and **work level**.

CALORIE BURN UP

The average daily energy intake from food for a man is 3500 calories, and for a woman 2500 calories, of which 10% is protein, 40% is fat and 50% is carbohydrates. However, the amount of energy that you actually need each day depends on many factors, such as body size, weight, and how much active exercise you do. If you take in more calories than you need, the excess will be stored as fat and your weight will increase.

To burn up extra calories, vigorous, **aerobic** activity involving the whole body is required. Exercising on a rowing machine is excellent for this purpose, because it is a concentrated movement, which works all the main muscles. For example, if exercising on a machine for 5 minutes at an average rowing rate, a man will burn up in the region of 80 calories, a woman around 60 calories.

Steps 1 & 3

PREPARE, PULL, & PUSH

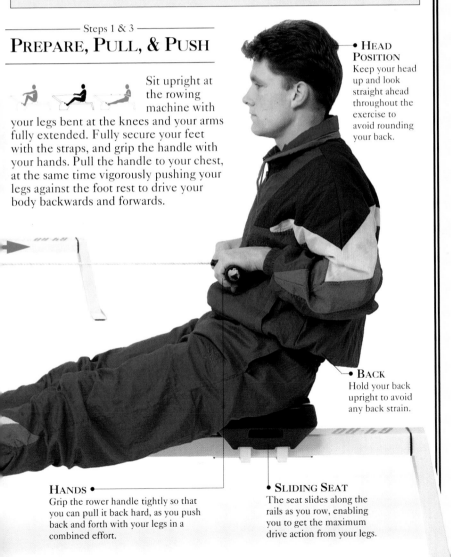

Sit upright at the rowing machine with your legs bent at the knees and your arms fully extended. Fully secure your feet with the straps, and grip the handle with your hands. Pull the handle to your chest, at the same time vigorously pushing your legs against the foot rest to drive your body backwards and forwards.

• **HEAD POSITION**
Keep your head up and look straight ahead throughout the exercise to avoid rounding your back.

• **BACK**
Hold your back upright to avoid any back strain.

HANDS •
Grip the rower handle tightly so that you can pull it back hard, as you push back and forth with your legs in a combined effort.

• **SLIDING SEAT**
The seat slides along the rails as you row, enabling you to get the maximum drive action from your legs.

ALL BODY STRETCH

*This stretching and bending movement gets your circulation going as well as exercising most of the major muscle groups. Rating •• *

• **EYES FRONT**
Stand up straight and keep your eyes fixed on your hands on the wall.

HANDS •
Your hands need to touch the wall, and then the floor, during the upright and crouched positions.

WALL SUPPORT •
Choose an empty wall, or a door that opens towards you, to give you the necessary support at the start of the exercise.

• **FEET**
Place your feet a shoulder's width apart, and remember to keep them rooted to the spot throughout the stretch movement.

Steps 1 & 2
HOLD AND BEND

Start off in an upright position about 60cm (2ft) away from a wall or a door. Place the flat of your palms on the wall at about your head height to gauge your distance. Slowly crouch down, bending your knees, and bring your arms forward.

• **ARM SWING**
Your arms drive downwards towards the floor, at the same time as your knees bend.

• **STOMACH TENSION**
The crouching action will cause the stomach muscles to tense, but the main pressure will be in the arms and legs.

• **KNEES**
Your knees start to bend fully into the crouch position. Without pausing, you bend down quickly and smoothly to touch the floor.

WARMED-UP MUSCLES

THE POSITIVE RESULTS
The benefits received from warming up
muscles before you start your full weight-
training workout, are well worth the time
spent on the initial exercises.
• You get more available energy as the
temperature of the muscles is raised and
the oxygen supply to them is increased.
• Your actions are more powerful because
your muscles move more quickly.
• The muscles and the movement of the
joints become much more flexible.
• Muscle co-ordination is much improved.

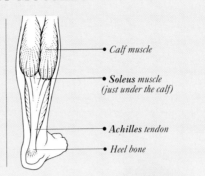

• *Calf muscle*

• **Soleus** *muscle*
(just under the calf)

• **Achilles** *tendon*

• *Heel bone*

Steps 3 & 4
CROUCH AND PUSH UP

Bend down fully to touch
the floor, and then push
upwards vigorously to
stretch the body back into an upright
position to begin again. The actions
need to be carried out rhythmically,
and quite fast, with even breathing
to get the maximum benefit for the
body. Repeat the exercise 4 times.

HEAD •
Your head remains in
natural alignment with
the body throughout
the stretching-up
exercise.

• **REACH**
After touching
the floor, your
arms come out
in front again
on the way up.

CONCENTRATION •
As you crouch down,
concentrate on the
floor before
springing
up again.

• **THIGHS**
Most of the
force you apply
on the way up
in the stretch
action, comes
from your leg
muscles. Do
not swing the
arms straight
up or put strain
on your back
muscles.

• **KNEES BENT**
This is one exercise in
which you can bend your
knees below a 90° angle,
provided you do not
suffer from any
injury problems.

• **BALANCE**
Place both your
hands on the floor
before pushing
yourself up again.

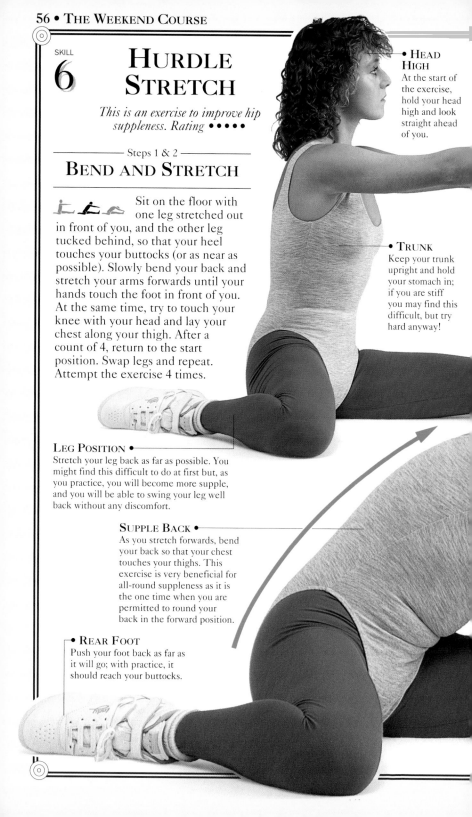

HURDLE STRETCH

This is an exercise to improve hip suppleness. Rating ● ● ● ●

———— Steps 1 & 2 ————
BEND AND STRETCH

Sit on the floor with one leg stretched out in front of you, and the other leg tucked behind, so that your heel touches your buttocks (or as near as possible). Slowly bend your back and stretch your arms forwards until your hands touch the foot in front of you. At the same time, try to touch your knee with your head and lay your chest along your thigh. After a count of 4, return to the start position. Swap legs and repeat. Attempt the exercise 4 times.

• HEAD HIGH
At the start of the exercise, hold your head high and look straight ahead of you.

• TRUNK
Keep your trunk upright and hold your stomach in; if you are stiff you may find this difficult, but try hard anyway!

LEG POSITION •
Stretch your leg back as far as possible. You might find this difficult to do at first but, as you practice, you will become more supple, and you will be able to swing your leg well back without any discomfort.

SUPPLE BACK •
As you stretch forwards, bend your back so that your chest touches your thighs. This exercise is very beneficial for all-round suppleness as it is the one time when you are permitted to round your back in the forward position.

• REAR FOOT
Push your foot back as far as it will go; with practice, it should reach your buttocks.

• ARMS

Stretch your arms out in front, parallel with your leg, and point your fingers towards your toes. As you do this you will feel your shoulder blades rotating forwards. Slowly lower your trunk and reach for your foot with your hands, keeping your arms taut.

— STRETCHING —

THE BENEFITS

General **warm-up** exercises help get the body ready for your weight-training session, but if more **repetitions** were undertaken for a longer time they could:
• Help improve the blood circulation
• Help reduce weight.

Trunk twist

Ski jump

Squat thrust

Hurdle stretch

Push-up

• FRONT LEG

Stretch your front leg out in a straight line in front of your body, and point your toes upwards towards the ceiling.

FULL STRETCH •

To achieve the maximum benefit from the stretch, hold on to your foot with both hands if possible.

HEAD •

Bring your head down as far as it will go, and hold it there for about 4 seconds.

SQUAT THRUST

*An all-body exercise that raises the **pulse rate** and improves coordination prior to the weight-training **program**. Rating • • • •*

—————— Steps 1-2 ——————

STAND UP AND CROUCH

The **squat thrust** is a fast, vigorous **warm-up** exercise, which should be performed continuously. Speak to yourself quietly throughout all of the exercise. By repeating quickly: "Down, feet back, forwards, up", you will remind yourself of each stage, and the quicker you speak, the faster you need to react. Ensure there's plenty of room behind you to perform all the movements. Stand with your feet together and eyes looking ahead. Keep your arms by your side with your palms resting on your thighs. Bend down vigorously to the floor until your body is in the full crouch position, with knees bent, buttocks nearly touching your heels, and your palms flat on the floor.

• **ARMS**
Your arms need to be kept close to your side in both the start and finish position of this exercise.

• **EASY BREATHING**
In the crouch position, your head stays looking forwards to facilitate easy and rapid breathing.

• **LEG SUPPORT**
When crouching down, you balance forwards on your toes and your heels lift right off the floor. Your knees are bent with your calf muscles touching the **hamstrings**. There is no hesitation at this point, because you move straight on to the next phase.

• **HOLD FIRM**
Your feet are positioned close together, staying on the same spot in all except the extended leg position of the exercise.

• **FULL EXTENT**
Your legs are stretched out behind you.

VARYING THE WARM-UPS

A DIFFERENT ROUTINE

Once you've perfected the **warm-ups** detailed, you might well feel like adding in some different stretching exercises to your normal workout routine, so that you do not become bored.

• LUNGES

Stand upright, keeping your feet apart. Take a large step forwards with your right leg, bending the knee so that it is above the right foot. Put your right hand on your knee and go down into the bent position so that you can feel the stretch in the muscles of your extended left leg. Change to the other leg. Repeat 4 times.

• SHOULDER LIFTS

Stand with feet apart and hands by your side, and lift your shoulders as high as they will go. Slowly lower them right down again, bending your knees at the same time. Keep all the movements very smooth and fluid. Repeat 4 times.

Steps 3-4

EXTEND AND PUSH UP

 From the crouch position, you shoot your legs out far behind you. Briefly you are in the **push-up** position with your head in alignment with your body for easy breathing. Your trunk and legs are fully stretched out, with your arms perpendicularly under your shoulders, supporting your body. Hold briefly, then shoot your legs forwards again back into the crouch position and drive your body upwards back to the start position. Attempt the exercise 4 times.

• STRAIGHT BACK
In this phase, you do the **push-up** stance, with your back forming a straight line through the hips to your ankles.

UPWARD STANCE •
As you come back up from the **push-up** position, your back is rounded to lessen strain on the back muscles, and your arms hang freely in front of your body. Slowly straighten up and return to the start position with your palms resting back on your thighs.

BALANCE •
Your hands are flat on the floor and your arms tense to support your body.

MOVING UPWARDS •
As you return upright, your legs work hard, pushing the body upwards before crouching again.

SKILL
6

HALF SQUAT

*A **warm-up** exercise for the leg and back muscles, which is done on a fixed-weight machine. Rating •••*

Steps 1-2

HOLD AND BEND

 Set a medium weight so that you meet **resistance,** but can comfortably raise the bar without straining. Stand with your back to the bar and grip the handles at shoulder level. Keep your back straight and head up as you bend down, slowly until your knees are at 90°. This is an exercise that can easily be done on a home fitness center.

SQUAT MACHINE •
The machine uses the **pulley** system to lift the amount of weight you've selected for the exercise.

• ARM POWER
Grip the handles underneath, and prepare the arms to take the strain.

• LEG SUPPORT
Keep your legs straight and both your feet slightly apart as you grip the **half-squat** bar.

• HIPS
Your hips are in alignment with your shoulders and ankles.

TENSE THIGHS •
Your thighs tense to take the strain as you slowly bend your legs. Keep your feet a slight distance apart to prevent any buckling at the knees.

Step 3

PUSH UP

When your knees are bent, hold for 2 seconds, then breathe in strongly and push the bar back up until your knees are straight and **locked**. It is now that you get the most benefit, so stop briefly before descending again. Attempt 4 times.

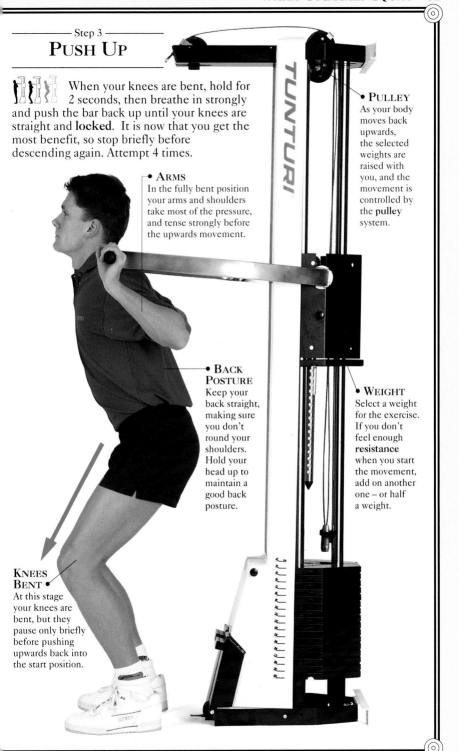

• PULLEY
As your body moves back upwards, the selected weights are raised with you, and the movement is controlled by the **pulley** system.

• ARMS
In the fully bent position your arms and shoulders take most of the pressure, and tense strongly before the upwards movement.

• BACK POSTURE
Keep your back straight, making sure you don't round your shoulders. Hold your head up to maintain a good back posture.

• WEIGHT
Select a weight for the exercise. If you don't feel enough **resistance** when you start the movement, add on another one – or half a weight.

KNEES BENT •
At this stage your knees are bent, but they pause only briefly before pushing upwards back into the start position.

SKILL

DAY 2

7

ARMS

Definition: A variety of exercises that work the upper body

EXERCISING WITH **FREE WEIGHTS** or machines increases the strength of your arm and shoulder muscles. Although floor exercises, such as **push-ups,** help; exercises with **barbells, dumbbells,** or **fixed-weight machines** ensure that you see a fast improvement.

OBJECTIVE: To further tone the arm and shoulder muscles.

BICEPS CURL

*A **barbell** lift movement to improve the upper arm and shoulder muscles. Rating ••*

——— Steps 1-2 ———
HOLD AND LIFT

— Lift up the **barbell** with both hands, bend your arms upwards, lifting it higher until it just touches your chest. Hold for a few seconds then lower slowly. Repeat 4 times.

• **SHOULDERS**
In this exercise your shoulders take the full strain of the weight, and they must be kept very rigid throughout the entire movement.

• **ARMS**
Keep your arms straight and by your side, with the insides of your elbows pointing forwards.

GRIP •
Using both hands, hold the **barbell** in an **undergrasp**, so that your palms are facing uppermost. In this position, you will be able to lift the barbell easily with little risk of dropping it.

• **LEGS**
Slowly bend your knees to pick up the **barbell**, then straighten them as you start to lift it up to your thighs.

• **FEET**
For a balanced position, keep the soles and heels of your feet flat on the floor, throughout the exercise.

DUMBBELL CURLS

On first impression this exercise may look a lot easier than the **biceps curl** action, but because each arm is holding a separate **dumbbell**, your weaker arm just cannot rely on the other one to help it out when it begins to gets tired.

RAISE RIGHT ARM
Standing upright, hold a **dumbbell** in each hand. Raise your right arm slowly, bringing the dumbbell right up to your chest, while resting the other one gently on your thigh.

LOWER & RAISE
Slowly lower your right arm again, while at the same time raising your left arm in a smooth, rhythmic movement.

RAISE LEFT ARM
When your right arm is lowered to your thigh, your left arm should be raised so that the **dumbbell** is level with your chest. Repeat 4 times.

• **TUCKED ARMS**
As you raise your arms to lift the **barbell** to your chest, keep your elbows tucked into your sides.

• **TORSO**
Although this exercise is good mainly for your arms and shoulders, your torso is also being toned by maintaining a really upright position without any bending backwards.

ARM MUSCLES

The biceps curl works the **biceps** and the **brachialis** muscles, but the **deltoids** and other shoulder muscles are also strengthened. Doing this exercise will not result in bulging muscles; these will only occur if you do **body-building** exercises.

Deltoids •
Biceps brachialis •

•*Triceps*

SKILL
7

BUTTERFLY MACHINE

*Increase the strength of the upper arms, **pectorals**, and upper back muscles with these arm swinging movements. Rating •••.*

———— Steps 1-2 ————
GRIP AND HOLD

ARM SWING •
As you press the pads inwards, you must ensure that the pressure is coming from your arms and shoulders and not just the forearms, which are touching the pads. It is a **dynamic tension** movement.

Set a moderate weight and adjust the seat. Keep your elbows at an angle of 90° and your forearms resting along the pads. Hold your head back and feet firm on the foot plate or floor (depending on machine). Tense, and press hard on the pads to force them towards each other in the center.

• SHOULDER STRENGTH
As you begin to tense your body to bring the forearms to the front, you will feel the pressure affecting the upper arms, **pectorals,** and also the upper back muscles.

• FOOT HOLD
By putting pressure on the foot plate with your feet, you'll find it easier to push.

• PAD PROTECTION
These pads help to reduce
any discomfort felt when
you push hard on them
with your forearms.

Step 3

SWING OUT

As you bring the pads
together, tense your
body and take a deep
breath, slowly letting it out as the
pads meet. Hold the pads briefly
in the front position, then breathe
in while you slowly let the cable
pulley take the pressure off you
and return the pads to the start
position. Always remember to
keep your head firmly back, and
against the seat, to prevent any
accidents. Attempt the exercise
4 times with a moderate weight.

• ARM TENSION
Your arms will tense the most
as the pads meet in the middle,
but will relax again on the return
movement to the start position.

SMOOTH MOVEMENT
The elbows are held at right
angles to the upper arms to
ensure a smooth action, and
an unrestricted blood supply.

LAT PULL-DOWN MACHINE

A pull-down movement behind the neck, which helps to tone the arm and back muscles. Rating • • •

--- Steps 1 & 2 ---
HOLD AND PULL

Select a light weight at the back of the machine and sit comfortably on the bench. Looking straight ahead, reach high to grasp the bar above your head, and plant your feet on the floor. To start, sit upright, tense your body and take in a deep breath. Grip the bar and pull down to your head while you exhale. On some larger machines it is possible to stand up to do the exercise.

• PULLEY SYSTEM
As you pull the bar down the weights are lifted by the **pulley** system. Keep the movements smooth and controlled or the weights will jerk up and down.

• ARM POWER
As you pull the bar further down your arms start to bend, forcing the elbows out, and you start to feel the tension in your stomach.

ARM MUSCLES •
The *Biceps brachialis* and **brachialis** are mainly used when the arms flex to pull the bar downwards. The lower arm muscles are also brought into play by the hands firmly gripping the bar.

FEET •
Point your feet forwards and keep them flat on the floor. If you're using a heavier weight, you must resist the tendency to lift your feet off the ground.

Step 3
STRETCH OUT

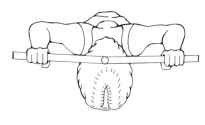

Finally, pull the bar right down behind the neck, making your arms bend and pushing your elbows out. Slowly release the bar. After the pull-down, there is a pause before the arms start to control the bar, because the weight pulls the bar upwards. If you hold the bar in front of the body, it becomes a **triceps** exercise. Attempt 4 times.

MUSCLE STRENGTHENING
As the bar is pulled down right behind the neck, you can clearly feel the strengthening process by how taut the hard working arm and back muscles are in action.

MUSCLE EFFECT •
To tone the back muscles, the bar is pulled down behind the neck. To affect the chest muscles the bar is pulled right down in front of the chest.

LEG SUPPORT •
Your legs must be motionless, even though you feel you are being pulled up by the exercise.

PULLEY SYSTEM •
As you pull the bar right down to the level of your shoulders, the **stack** of weights is lifted halfway up the machine by the cable **pulley** system.

PULL-DOWN BAR •
The bar is attached to the moving cable, which permits lateral and vertical movement during all stages of the arm exercise.

8

TRUNK

Definition: *Exercises for the abdomen and lower-back muscles.*

WHEN EXERCISING YOUR TRUNK AREA, be careful not to strain your back muscles. Keep your back straight and bend your legs when lifting weights, or you may develop a curved back.

OBJECTIVE: To increase strength in the back and **abdominal** area.

DEAD LIFT

A simple exercise that increases the mobility of the powerful thigh, hip, and lower-back muscles. Rating ••

——— Step 2 ———
LIFT AND LOWER

Lift the **barbell** off the **rack** or the floor, then slowly bring it up to thigh height. Hold for a count of 4 and lower it down again. Remember to keep your back straight. Repeat the action 4 times.

• SHOULDERS AND BACK
Hold your shoulders rigid and keep your back very straight, allowing your legs to do most of the hard work.

ARM POSITION •
Keep your arms straight, while holding the **barbell** with an under-arm or over-arm grip.

STANCE •
Stand with both your feet a shoulder's width apart, and your toes pointing forwards. Bend your legs to pick up the **barbell**, then straighten them to lift it. Keep your feet still throughout the exercise.

TRUNK ROTATION

*Twisting the upper part of the body while holding a **barbell**, to strengthen the back and **abdominal** muscles. Rating • •*

• BARBELL POSITION
Rest the **barbell** across your shoulders and back of your neck, and grip it near the **collars** so that your elbows are bent. To relieve pressure along your shoulders, wrap a towel around the barbell.

SHOULDERS •
Keep your shoulders straight, supporting the weight of the **barbell**, while you rotate your trunk from side to side.

LEGS AND FEET •
Stand with your feet apart and keep your legs straight, but not too rigid at the knees. Do not try to move your feet even when you twist all of your upper body.

TRUNK •
Keep your back and abdomen straight, so that as you rotate you build up a slow, steady rhythm and your movements do not become jerky.

— Steps 1-2 —

STAND AND TURN

Ask a partner to help you lift the weighted **barbell** onto your shoulders. Stand with your legs apart, supporting the barbell. Keeping your feet still, slowly turn your upper body to one side until you are facing sideways. Pause, and rotate to face the other way. This rotation is mainly from the hips, but a slight tension will be felt at your knees. Repeat 4 times with a light weight.

BACK EXTENSION

SKILL
8

This exercise involves stretching your back to increase the flexibility of your **Latissimus dorsi** *and* **trapezius** *muscles. Rating* • • • •

• **BACK**
To avoid back strain, keep it straight all the time. Hold your head in line with your back and don't let it drop forwards.

Steps 1 & 2
PREPARE AND LIFT

Adjust the pad and place your feet on the base, with your heels against its back to stop any movement. Press the backs of your hands against your forehead, breathe in very deeply and, with a rigid back, lift your body up to the horizontal position.

• **ARMS**
Hold your arms up to your head and place the backs of your hands against your forehead; then you can put your hands on the floor when you become tired.

• **LEGS**
Keep your legs rigid and your feet planted on the base of the machine. Here your legs act as **fixators**, **anchoring** your body, and must not be moved at any stage.

HORIZONTAL BACK •
Inhale deeply, lift your head backwards and push your elbows back to help raise your body slowly, until your back is in this horizontal position. Remember to keep your back rigid while you are lifting your whole body upwards, so that all of your back muscles feel taut and stretched.

STOMACH MUSCLES •
During the raising movement your **abdominals** become taut, preventing a rounded back.

Step 3
RAISE AND LOWER

Continue raising yourself up slowly until your head is in alignment with your body. Sustain this position for a count of 4, then exhale slowly while lowering yourself down gently until you reach the start position once more. Repeat the exercise 4 times.

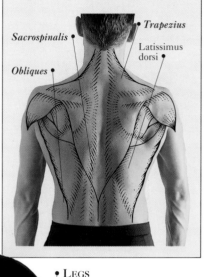

BACK MUSCLES

This exercise helps to strengthen the back muscles. With regular practice, your endurance will increase. To define your back muscles further, lift weights while raising your body; the heavier the weights, the greater the definition.

Trapezius

Sacrospinalis

Latissimus dorsi

Obliques

• HEAD
At the highest position of the movement your head and back are in natural alignment with your body. Hold for a count of 4.

CHEST •
By holding your arms up by your head and away from your chest, your ribs are stretched wide apart, which helps you to breathe deeply in and out.

• LEGS
The muscles at the back of your legs – which include the **gluteals, hamstrings,** and calf muscles – are stretched tight and working very hard in this final position of the exercise.

STOMACH •
In this position your **abdominal** muscles are fully tensed; this ensures that you do not fall too quickly in the lowering action of the movement.

SKILL
8

DUMBBELL SIDE BENDS

*This stretching exercise involves bending from side to side with a **dumbbell** in one hand, to strengthen the side, spine and **abdominal** muscles. Rating • •*

• RIGHT ARM
Hold your right arm up
and bend it so that your
hand is behind
your head.

——— Steps 1 & 2 ———
BEND AND LEAN

 Stand upright with your legs apart. Hold your right hand behind your head, and grip a weighted **dumbbell** in your left hand. Let the weight pull you down to the left side until your right side is fully stretched. Then bend slowly to the right, hold the position for a count of 2, pulling the weight up as you go. Breathe in while raising the weight, and out while lowering it.

**• LEFT
HAND**
Hold a
dumbbell
in your left
hand, close to
your thigh.

TRUNK •
Keep your trunk
straight throughout
the exercise. As you
bend sideways, be
careful not to lean
backwards or
forwards, as this
could strain your
side and back
muscles.

• FEET
Stand with your feet a shoulder's
width apart for a well-balanced
position to support your body.

• **LEFT ARM**
Hold your left
arm up so that
your hand is
pressed against
the back of your
head. This will
help you to stop
leaning forward,
while slowly
bending
sideways.

Steps 3 & 4

STRETCH AND BEND

Swap the **dumbbell**
over and change your
arm positions. This time, bend fully to
the right until you feel the muscles of
your side really stretching, then bend
sideways to the left. Return to the
start position and repeat the exercise 4
times on each side. Take care when
doing the movements that you keep
them smooth and don't bang the
dumbbell against your thigh.

— BARBELL BENDS —

SIDE AND BACK EXERCISES
To achieve the same effect on the side
and back muscles, try bending while
holding a **barbell** behind the neck.
This exercise is good for both men
and women. It is important to
tighten up the **collars** of the
barbell so that the weight **discs**
are held firmly in position.

*Stand with legs
apart and the
barbell across
your shoulders.*

*Lean over to the
right, as far as
you can go.*

• **TRUNK**
Bend over to
the left until
you feel a
stretching
sensation
along the
length of
your sides
and between
your ribs.
Hold for a
count of 2
before
returning
to the start
position.

*Stand up straight
again, then bend
down to the left.*

LEGS

DAY 2

Definition: *Exercises for the extensor and flexor muscles*

YOU CAN EXERCISE YOUR LEGS USING either **fixed-weight machines** or **free weights,** but the advantage of using weight machines is that they are targeted at improving specific groups of muscles. On the other hand, it can be more difficult when exercising with free weights to devise the type of exercises that specifically help to strengthen your leg muscles.

OBJECTIVE: To further improve leg muscles.

LEG EXTENSION

An exercise designed to strengthen the front muscles of the leg.
Rating ● ●

• LEGS
Dangle your legs loosely over the edge of the seat, so that your feet do not touch the floor, and push the front of your ankles against the pads of the **leg extension** unit, ready to lift it up.

WEIGHTS & PULLEY •
Insert the appropriate weight in the weight **stack**. The weight should be enough to produce a slight **resistance** when you lift up the leg unit. Start with a light weight and then progress to heavier weights. When you lift the leg unit with your legs, a cable in the **pulley** system pulls the selected weight up into the air.

• GRIP
Grip the side handles of the machine firmly with both hands throughout all the leg stretching movements.

LEG CURL

Many leg exercises often neglect the **hamstring** muscles at the back of the leg, and concentrate simply on strengthening the front leg muscles, such as the thighs or **quadriceps**. The **leg curl** exercise is an ideal **flexion** exercise for developing the hamstring muscles as it can often be done on the same machine as the **leg extension** exercise.

breathing out as you lift. Hold briefly, then slowly lower the weight while breathing in again. Select lighter weights than those used in the leg extension exercise. Attempt 4 times.

HOOK AND LIFT
Lie on your stomach on the flat seat of the machine and rest your chin on the surface. Rest your arms in front and hook both legs under the leg unit. Take a deep breath and lift your legs upwards, raising the leg unit towards your buttocks,

Steps 1 & 3
PREPARE AND LIFT

Sit on the machine, leaning against the back rest and grip the handles firmly. Press the front of your ankles against the leg unit and slowly raise it up by stretching your legs out in front of you. Breathe in before you begin and then exhale as you straighten your legs. Hold for a few seconds before lowering your legs down again. Attempt the exercise 4 times.

• **SEAT**
Adjust the seat and backrest so you can sit in a comfortable position with your head relaxed.

LEG EXTENSION UNIT •
As you raise your legs to lift the leg unit, this tightens the cable in the **pulley**, which then lifts all the weights in the weight **stack**.

LEGS •
In this position, all the effort of lifting the leg unit is focused on the muscles at the front of your legs.

SKILL

9

HIP MACHINE

*A movement to develop the shape of the **adductor** and **abductor** muscles. Rating • •*

• LEG MOVEMENT

As the right leg presses against the pad and swings back and forth you are helping to strengthen the three sets of **adductor** muscles: the **longus**, **magnus** and **brevis** on the inner thigh, which are also attached to the pelvic bone. Their main muscle action is to bring your legs from a sideways position back towards the body, and they also help to perform the grip action.

—————— Steps 1-2 ——————
PUSH IN AND OUT

Set a light weight and then adjust the platform. Stand very upright and grasp the machine's handle. Keep your left leg motionless on the platform and, with your right leg held very tense against the pad, push it inwards as far as you can reach before returning to the start position. Change over legs and work the left leg.

• SUPPORT
The left leg remains firm during the leg swinging movement, preventing the body from swaying during the exerted effort.

PUSH OUT AND IN

To work the outer **abductor** muscles, stand upright on the platform in exactly the same position as for the inner thigh movement. The main difference is that you place your right leg on the outside of the pad and the force of the movement is exerted outwards as far as you can go. Change legs to work the left leg. Keep the motion slow and smooth to get the maximum benefit from the exercise. Attempt all movements 4 times.

• OUTER LEG
During this leg exercise, it is imperative that you keep your whole body rigid by gripping the bar firmly with your hands. Also push down hard on the platform with the leg that's not moving to maintain a good balance. All the muscles in the working leg are rigid and therefore get some beneficial effect from the back and forth action. However, it is the muscles along the outside of the thigh that will tone up and improve the most.

•GRIP
On this exercise machine, your hands grip the front bar.

• HIP ACTION
The swinging action of the legs also helps to firm them up and give more definition to the shape of your hips.

STEP-ON-BENCH EXERCISE

*A **free-weights** exercise, which uses a stepping-on movement to develop the thigh muscles. Rating* • • •

--- Steps 1-2 ---
STEP UP AND ON

This is an alternative to the **half squat** exercise (see pp.46-47) and the leg press machine (see pp.44-45). Choose a light weight and use your partner to help you place the chosen **barbell** along your shoulders so that you can start in an upright position. Stand in front of a firm bench about 38cm (15in) high. Look straight ahead, and try not to sway, as you step onto the bench with the right leg, immediately followed by the left.

• SHOULDERS
Press your shoulders well back and hold the **barbell** near the **collars**. Wrap a towel around the bar to protect tender muscles. Don't twist your body as you step on and off the bench.

• TRUNK
Make sure your trunk is straight and upright as you step onto the bench.

• HEAD SENSE
Your head position is critical in this exercise, because it can prevent any buckling in your back. Keep your chin up and your eyes looking slightly above your head height.

• STEPPING ACTION
The stepping leg does most of the work, and because of the **barbell** there will be a tendency to wobble. Make it a slow, deliberate movement as you drive upwards to prevent the body going ahead of the leg.

• REAR LEG
Your rear leg needs to hold firm until the stepping leg is on the bench.

• BENCH
For this exercise try and use a wooden, unpadded surface. A height of about 38cm (15in) is best, but beginners can use a lower height.

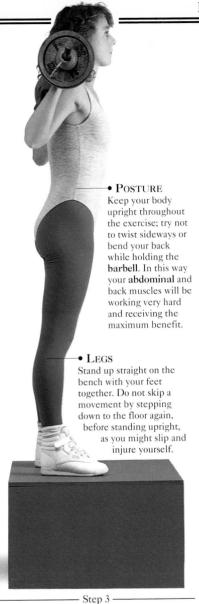

• **POSTURE**
Keep your body
upright throughout
the exercise; try not
to twist sideways or
bend your back
while holding the
barbell. In this way
your **abdominal** and
back muscles will be
working very hard
and receiving the
maximum benefit.

• **LEGS**
Stand up straight on the
bench with your feet
together. Do not skip a
movement by stepping
down to the floor again,
before standing upright,
as you might slip and
injure yourself.

——— Step 3 ———
STEP DOWN

Stand on the bench
keeping both legs
together. Then step
off backwards placing your left leg
first. Change to your left leg so that
both legs are exercised equally.
Repeat 4 times, using a light weight.

CALF RAISE

A **free-weights** exercise to
strengthen the calf muscles
of the leg. Repeat 4 times
holding a light weight.

**HEELS
DOWN**
Stand with
your heels
on the floor
and your
toes on a
weight **disc.**
Support a
barbell
on your
shoulders.

HEELS UP
Stand on your toes
on the block, count to
4 slowly, then lower
your heels to the floor.

MUSCLES

Regular weight training will help to
strengthen and tone the main muscles
of your thighs and calves, namely the
gastrocnemius, **soleus** and the
Achilles tendon.

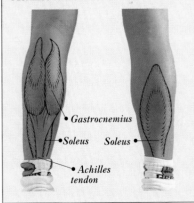

• *Gastrocnemius*

•*Soleus*   *Soleus* •

• *Achilles
tendon*

10 COOL-DOWNS

DAY 2

Definition: *Exercises to help your body slow down*

COOL-DOWN EXERCISES HELP TO disperse waste products that have built up during a workout. When you exercise, **glycogen** in the blood converts to **lactic acid**. If exercise stops abruptly, this remains in the exercised area and can cause muscle stiffness.

OBJECTIVE: To disperse the **lactic acid** built up in the blood from exercise, and facilitate recovery.

NECK SHRUGGING

*This upper-body action helps to lower the **pulse rate**. Rating •*

——— Steps 1-2 ———
UP AND DOWN

Put on your sweatsuit. Stand with your feet a shoulder's width apart and place hands on hips. Slowly drop your chin onto your chest. Then breathe in and slowly raise your head backwards so your chin is in the air and your neck is stretched. An alternative to this exercise is to turn your head slowly to the left and then to the right while shrugging your shoulders. Repeat 4 times.

HEAD MOVEMENTS
When lowering your head, concentrate on reducing both your breathing and **pulse rate**. When raising your head, do not attempt to lean so far back that it restricts your breathing.

STAIR MACHINE

*An **aerobic** exercise machine that enables you to walk on the spot against gentle **resistance**. Rating •*

--- Step 1-2 ---

PUSH DOWN AND UP

Stand on the machine, planting your feet firmly on the steps, and hold onto the side rails. Set the machine to a low **resistance** level. Keep your body upright and push down alternately with both feet, as if you were climbing stairs. Perform four "steps" with each leg. This exercise will help you regain control of your breathing and **pulse rate**.

PULSE •
A pulse-taking device, which looks rather like a thimble, is wired up to the machine to show you the lowering level of your **pulse rate**.

• **DISPLAY**
Keep your eyes fixed on the **digital read-out** while you exercise.

• **LEGS**
The walking movement on the stair machine is like steadily walking up stairs. Equal effort should be exerted by each leg and there should be no jerky body movements.

EASTERN PRAYER

SKILL

10 *A **cool-down** exercise to assist in lowering the pulse rate. Rating* • •

• **FEET**
Point your toes out behind you.

FULL OUT •
From the knees downwards, your legs and feet remain in virtually the same stretched-out position throughout the exercise. But your upper legs and buttocks move up, pause to crouch, and then go backwards until your buttocks push firmly against the back of your heels.

LEGS •
As you push up into the crouch position your arms and thighs give the main support. There's hardly a pause before your legs move backwards.

• **ROUNDED BACK**
Here your head tucks right in as the whole body moves backwards. Your back becomes fully rounded, and the movement really helps to stretch out the back muscles.

• BUTTOCKS
The buttocks play an important part in the pushing back action in the initial phase of the exercise.

• HEAD
Make sure your head is facing downwards in a straight line with your body throughout all the movements.

• ARM POWER
Your arms start in a **push-up** position, but keep your hands nearer your waist than your shoulders. A vigorous initial push action starts the movement by raising the body from the floor and the continuing pushing effort brings it up to hold the fully crouched position.

• CONTROLLED BREATHING
When lying flat on the stomach, a deep breath is taken, and as the arms push you right up, start to breathe out through your mouth during the releasing backwards movement. A deep breath is taken as the body returns to the lying position, and exhaled slowly. Always breathe evenly throughout all the exercise **repetitions**.

FLAT PALMS •
The palms of your hands stay flat on the mat during all the exercise movements, but help to give the most body support during the strenuous **push-up** phase.

Steps 1-3

PUSH UP AND CURL

As its name suggests, this **cool-down** exercise resembles the low kneeling position adopted by people praying to Mecca in Eastern countries. To begin, lie down on your stomach on a mat on the floor. Bend your arms, keeping your hands flat on the floor. Take a deep breath and push hard on your arms so that the upper half of your body begins to move upwards and backwards while you start to breathe out. Continue pushing back until your buttocks touch your heels, stretch your arms out in front of you and assume a tight, curled position with your head tucked well in to your body. Pause for a few seconds, then take another deep breath, and breathe out while you gradually return to the stretched-out start position. The action is carried out in a slow, sustained movement. Attempt the exercise 4 times.

AFTER THE WEEKEND

Joining a gym and getting a fitness program

NOW THAT YOU HAVE COMPLETED YOUR introductory weekend, you need to plan for the future. If you find you're keen on weight training have a look at the gym at your local sports center. They normally charge an annual fee plus a small amount per session. Often an induction course is included and the instructor will show you how to use the equipment. Alternatively you can join a health club, which is more expensive but they have more facilities. When you join you'll get a fitness assessment and a **program** will be worked out to suit your needs. To keep fit, 20 minutes of exercise per day is sufficient but two or three slightly longer sessions per week are adequate. One or two of these could be weight training with the other session being another sport such as swimming.

PROGRAM PLANNING

For each weight-training session, try and do about 6 exercises after your initial **warm-ups.** From your **program** do the basic exercises (1 arm and shoulder, 1 trunk and 1 leg exercise) plus 2 or 3 supplementary exercises to strengthen specific muscles.

WARM-UPS •
A good 10 minutes should always be spent on warming up the muscles before the main weight-training session.

BASIC EXERCISES •
These form the main core of your **program;** the extra ones can be changed to suit you.

• WEIGHTS
The weights you lift will be low at first, but will increase as you get fitter.

• SETS
If your own **program** says that you should do 3 **sets** x 10 **repetitions,** it means that you do an exercise 30 times, with a pause between each set of 10.

• REPETITIONS
A **repetition** equals the number of times that you must do an exercise, so if your **program** says 10 repetitions, you do the exercise 10 times.

COOL-DOWNS •
These bring pulse and temperature back to normal after a workout.

PERSONAL EXERCISE PROGRAM

Name	Timothy Jones							
Date								
5/91								

Activity				
Aerobic weight training				

		Freq.	Days
Warm-ups		Sets & reps.	2 or 3
Warm-up stretching exercises: 5 minutes			
Aerobic exercise bike: 6 minutes, level 10			

No.	Exercise	Wt kg	Reps	Sets
	Basic – 1 kg			
1	Bench press			
2	Trunk twist			
3	Leg press			
	Supplementary	23	10	3
4	Biceps curl	nil	10	3
5	Lat pull-down	45	10	3
	Basic – 2 (5/6/91)			
1	Bench press	11	10	3
2	Trunk twist	9	10	3
3	Leg press			
	Supplementary	34	6	3
4	Calf raise	4.5	6	3
5	Hip machine	68	6	3
				3
		45	10	3
		11	10	3

Cool-downs
Aerobic rowing machine: 5 minutes, medium level
Cool-down exercises: 5 minutes

YOUR BODY

How it works and keeping it healthy

NOW THAT YOU'RE COMMITTED TO PERSEVERING with weight training, it is important that you find out a bit more about your body: how it works, what foods you need to eat and the effects that exercise has upon it. The body consists of bones to provide the rigid outer framework and cartilage (gristle), which acts as a cushion between the joints of the bones. Ligaments are tough, flexible tissues which hold the bones together. Muscles control body movement and consist of numerous fibers like bunches of human hair. Tendons are the strong bands of tissue forming the end of the fleshy part of muscles where they meet the bones.

TREATING AN INJURY

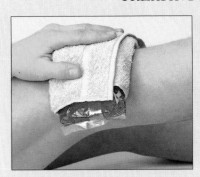 

HOW TO COPE
Normally, a good **warm-up** before weight training will prevent any injuries, but if a muscle injury does occur a cold compress should be applied immediately to stop the internal bleeding. The compress can be bought from a chemist, should be placed in the freezer, and then applied wrapped in a towel to the strained area. Lift the injured muscle right off the ground to relieve pressure as you apply the compress. The injury should be left for 24 hours after which your doctor or physiotherapist will recommend any further treatment they think necessary.

SERIOUS INJURIES
If you develop a serious muscle tear it will need immediate medical attention. A useful point to remember is that if there is a sharp pain in the muscle, it is normally a tear with internal bleeding. If it is merely a mild, dull ache it is probably only a minor pulled muscle, which will heal naturally.

MUSCLES

Muscles are given energy by the heart and lungs, which in turn increase the blood circulation and breathing to enable exercise to continue. If the heart and lungs cannot keep up with the muscles' needs, fatigue sets in and the muscles stop functioning until you rest. Muscle stiffness is due to waste products staying in the muscles. It will disappear after further exercise.

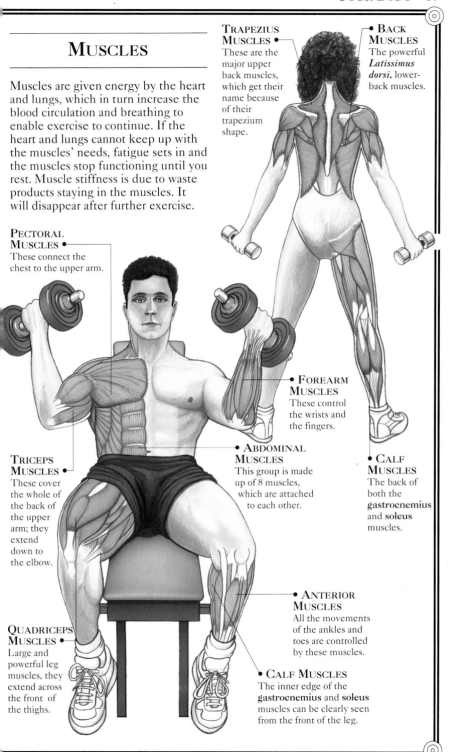

TRAPEZIUS MUSCLES • These are the major upper back muscles, which get their name because of their trapezium shape.

• BACK MUSCLES The powerful *Latissimus dorsi,* lower-back muscles.

PECTORAL MUSCLES • These connect the chest to the upper arm.

• FOREARM MUSCLES These control the wrists and the fingers.

TRICEPS MUSCLES • These cover the whole of the back of the upper arm; they extend down to the elbow.

• ABDOMINAL MUSCLES This group is made up of 8 muscles, which are attached to each other.

• CALF MUSCLES The back of both the **gastrocnemius** and **soleus** muscles.

QUADRICEPS MUSCLES • Large and powerful leg muscles, they extend across the front of the thighs.

• ANTERIOR MUSCLES All the movements of the ankles and toes are controlled by these muscles.

• CALF MUSCLES The inner edge of the **gastrocnemius** and **soleus** muscles can be clearly seen from the front of the leg.

A HEALTHY DIET

What you need to eat to keep in trim

WHEN YOU EXERCISE REGULARLY you need to watch your food intake to ensure you are eating the right amount of nutritional food and drink. Remember that regular exercise tones you up, but does not keep your weight down, it is up to you to control it. The main aims in a healthy diet are to reduce your fat and sugar intake. That means cutting down on: fried foods, cream, butter, red meat, chocolate and cakes, and reducing your sugar intake: cookies, pastries, sweetened fruit juices, soft drinks, and candy. Increase all the foods with low fat, high carbohydrates and fiber: chicken, oily fish, milk, fresh fruit and vegetables, beans, brown rice, wholemeal bread, and pasta. Try and keep your alcohol intake down to the recommended: 14 units a week for women and 21 for men.

• **GOOD MINERALS**
Bananas have practically no fat, but good levels of minerals and carbohydrate.

• **HIGH VITAMINS**
Carrots are high in vitamin A, which keeps the skin healthy. They can be eaten raw as snacks.

• **LOW-FAT**
Oily fish is low-fat; use it to replace red meat.

• **PROTEIN**
Cheese has a high vitamin, mineral, and protein content, and although high in fat, helps to provide high energy levels.

• **HIGH FIBER**
Beans provide the fiber needed in a healthy diet, and help prevent the digestive system becoming sluggish.

WEIGHT CHARTS

The calories needed to keep your body weight even depends on your sex, occupation, weight, and age. As a rough guide women need between 2000-2500 calories per day and men between 2700-3500. Older people need about 500 less. The charts below show average weights related to height, and the healthy-weight range covers small, medium, and large builds.

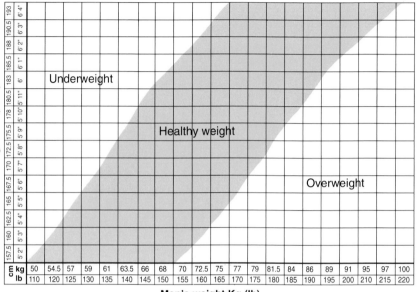

cm kg	50	54.5	57	59	61	63.5	66	68	70	72.5	75	77	79	81.5	84	86	89	91	95	97	100
lb	110	120	125	130	135	140	145	150	155	160	165	170	175	180	185	190	195	200	210	215	220

Men's weight Kg (lb)

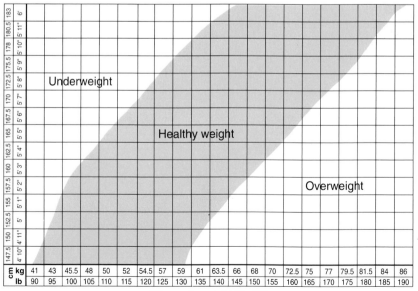

cm kg	41	43	45.5	48	50	52	54.5	57	59	61	63.5	66	68	70	72.5	75	77	79.5	81.5	84	86
lb	90	95	100	105	110	115	120	125	130	135	140	145	150	155	160	165	170	175	180	185	190

Women's weight Kg (lb)

FUTURE PROGRAMS

How to progress and improve

WHEN YOU FIRST START WEIGHT TRAINING you normally select a weight that can be lifted comfortably and then repeat the exercise ten times. After a few seconds' rest, you repeat the action ten times more, rest again, and do a final ten **repetitions** before moving onto the next exercise. This is written in your **program** (see p.85) as three **sets** of ten repetitions with x lb. This type of exercising increases endurance. To increase strength as well, extra weight needs to be added to the **barbell**, but the numbers of repetitions are reduced, so you do three sets of six repetitions with x plus 10lb. Gradually, the number of repetitions you do can be reduced further and the weight increased, for example, three sets of four repetitions with x plus 20lb. More advanced weight trainers use the special **pyramid** system described below.

THE PYRAMID SYSTEM

This system, which creates mainly a strengthening effect on the body is to be attempted by advanced weight trainers only. The usual **pyramid** system consists of 5, 6 or 7 reps of a light weight, then progressively the amount of weight is increased while reducing the repetitions by 1 until there is one final lift with a heavy weight to finish. Illustrated below is a **program** where the weight trainer would lift 90lb of weight **discs** 7 times, then 100lb 6 times until the final lift of 155lb is reached. The method requires maximum effort with a heavier weight when the muscles are just starting to get tired. Variations on this method include the reverse pyramid, where the first lift can be 155lb, for example, with the next 2 lifts being 145lb and so on. In both methods when you have successfully completed all the lifts, you then adjust the schedule to start all over again, this time with a heavier weight.

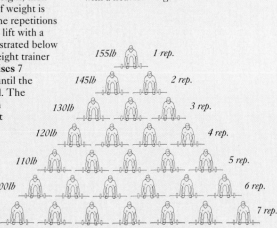

SPORTS PROGRAMS

Once you've been given the 3 basic exercises, the 2 or 3 supplementary ones added to your personal fitness **program** can be related to a specific sport, which you regularly play. But when devising a specific sports-related program you need always to remember that exercises must first be related to either strength or endurance requirements. Some typical examples are given below.

GOLF

The golf swing is an **anaerobic** exercise, but the game consists of walking over different terrain for hours, bringing in a certain amount of **aerobic** exercise.

EXERCISES
All body: Rowing machine (see p.52)
Arms & shoulders: Biceps curl with **dumbbells** (see p.62), Butterfly machine (see p.65)
Trunk: Trunk rotation (see p.69), **Back extension** (see p.70)
Legs: Recumbent leg press (see p.44).

TENNIS

A mixture of some **anaerobic** and **aerobic** work is required with tennis. Good development of strength, endurance and skill is also needed for this sport.

EXERCISES
All body: Exercise bicycle (see p.26), Stair machine (see p.81).
Arms & shoulders: Dumbbell punch (see p.39), Biceps curl (see p.62)
Trunk: Trunk twist (see p.42)
Legs: Half squat (see p.60), **Calf raise** (see p.79).

ROCK CLIMBING

This is mainly a dynamic strength activity with strong use of the arms and legs.

EXERCISES
All body: Dead lift (see p.68)
Arms & shoulders: Military press (see p.38), Butterfly machine (see p.64)
Trunk: Trunk twist (see p.42), **Back extension** (see p.70)
Legs: Leg press (see p.44), **Calf raise** (see p.79).

SKIING

This is an activity requiring strength and endurance. These can be increased by exercises using a mixture of heavy and light weights.

EXERCISES
All body: Exercise bicycle (see p. 26)
Arms & shoulders: Dumbbell punch (see p.39)
Trunk: Trunk rotation (see p.69), **Sit-ups** (see p.40)
Legs: Step-on-bench (see p.78), Leg press (see p.44) and Stair machine (see p.81).

GLOSSARY

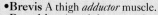

Words in *italic* are glossary entries.

A

- **Abdominal** A stomach muscle.
- **Abductor** A movement that moves a limb away from the body.
- **Achilles** A tendon joining the calf muscles to the heel bone.
- **Adductor** A movement that returns a limb near to the body.
- **Aerobic** Vigorous activity which makes heart and lungs work at full capacity.
- **All body stretch** A *warm-up* exercise to increase circulation.
- **Allen screw** A screw used to tighten collars on a barbell or a dumbbell.
- **Allen wrench** A wrench to tighten *dumbbell* or *Allen screws*.
- **Anchor** To hold down.
- **Anaerobic** Highly concentrated exercise, done in short bursts.
- **Arm rotation** A *warm-up* exercise for arms and shoulders.

B

- **Back extension** A trunk exercise.
- **Barbell** A length of steel bar onto which weight *discs* are loaded.
  - **Bench press** A *press* performed while lying supine on a bench.
  - **Biceps** An upper arm muscle.
  - **Biceps curl** A *barbell* movement to improve upper-arm muscles.
  - **Body-building** Program of exercises and diet to develop the muscles.
  - **Brachialis** An upper arm muscle.

- **Brevis** A thigh *adductor* muscle.
- **Breathing** A *cool-down* exercise to return the body to its normal state.

C

- **Cardiovascular endurance** Fitness training to keep the heart rate at a high level for a sustained period.
- **Clean lift** Raising a *barbell* from the floor to be held against the chest.
- **Collar** Plastic or cast-iron fixing to hold weight *discs* in place.
- **Cool-downs** Exercises to slow the body down after a vigorous workout.

D

- **Dead lift** Lifting a weighted *barbell* from the floor to hip height.
- **Deltoid** A shoulder muscle.
- **Digital read-out** An *aerobic* machine's electronic display.
- **Discs** These are weighted, and are added to *free weights*.
- **Dumbbell** Small bar with added weights, used for arm actions.
- **Dumbbell side bends** A stretching action for the side and stomach.
- **Dynamic tension** The whole body goes rigid as part of an exercise.

E

- **Eastern prayer** An all-body, *cool-down* exercise performed on the floor.
- **Extension** A stretching movement.
- **Extensor** Stretching foot muscle.

F

- **Fixators** Muscles that are taut, but which do not move.
- **Fixed-weight machines** Equipment to strengthen specific muscles.
- **Flexion** A bending movement.
- **Free weights** Weighted *barbells* and *dumbbells* for weight training.

G

- **Gastrocnemius** A calf muscle.
- **Gluteals** The buttock muscles.
- **Glycogen** Energy source of the blood.

H

- **Half squat** A *free-weight* exercise for the hips and thighs.
- **Hamstring** Muscle in back of the thigh.
- **Hurdle stretch** A *warm-up* exercise to improve hip flexibility.

I

- **Isotonic** Exercise which concentrates on specific muscles.

J

- **Jogging** A *cool-down* exercise that involves very slow running.
- **Jerk** A *barbell* lift above the head.

L

- **Lactic acid** Waste product found in the blood after exercising.
- *Latissimus dorsi* A back muscle.
- **Leg curl** A *fixed-weight machine* exercise for the *hamstring* muscles.
- **Leg extension** A leg action on a *fixed-weight machine*.
- **Locked** When arms or legs are completely extended.
- **Low-impact** A less strenuous form of exercise to reduce joint stress.
- **Longus** A thigh *adductor* muscle.

M

- **Magnus** An *adductor* muscle.
- **Military press** A movement that brings a *barbell* above the head.
- **Modified clean and jerk** A body stretch exercise with *free weights*.

N

- **Neck shrugging** A *cool-down* exercise to loosen tense shoulder muscles.

O

- **Oblique** A side muscle.

P

- **Pectorals** Upper chest muscles.
- **Press** To lift a *barbell* up and down above the head; to push on a machine.
- **Pulley** Grooved wheel to carry the cable system in *fixed-weight machine*s.
- **Pulse rate** The beats per minute that the heart pumps out blood.
- **Push-up** A floor exercise for the arms.

- **Pyramid** A system of organizing *repetitions* using different weights.

Q

- **Quadriceps** A front thigh muscle.

R

- **Rack** A piece of equipment to hold *barbell*s, *dumbbell*s, and weight *discs*.
- *Rectus abdominis* Stomach muscle.
- **Resistance** The pressure felt when a machine's work level is set.

S

- **Sacrospinalis** A spine muscle.
- **Set** The number of *repetitions* to do.
- **Sit-up** A stomach, floor exercise.
- **Sleeve** An attachment on a *barbell* or *dumbbell* to prevent hand strain.
- **Soleus** A calf muscle.
- **Squat thrust** A calisthenic exercise.
- **Stack** The pile of weight *discs* on a *fixed-weight machine*.
- **Step-on-bench exercise** A *free-weights* exercise for thighs.
- **Stress injury** Muscle or joint injury caused by over-training.
- **Stretch and curl** A *cool-down* exercise to reduce muscle tension.

T

- **Trapezius** The diamond-shaped back muscles.
- **Triceps** An arm muscle.
- **Trunk twist** A floor action for stomach muscles.

U

- **Undergrasp** Gripping a *barbell* from underneath.

W

- **Warm-up** Gentle exercising before a workout.
- **Weight station** A large gym machine for up to five people.
- **Work level** A set pace rate.

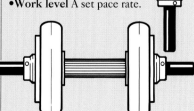

INDEX

ACKNOWLEDGMENTS

Dr Nick Whitehead and Dorling Kindersley would like to thank the following
for their help in the production of this book:

Rick Kiddle and Sally Iken for their modeling and helpful suggestions.
Collard and Company PR on behalf of Olympus Sport for the loan of their
exercise bike and clothing.
PR Solutions on behalf of DP Products for the loan of their bench press
and weight-training accessories.
BH Fitness for the loan of their Tunturi home fitness center.
Gym 80 for the loan of their fixed gym machines.
R.A.T. (Manufacturing) Limited for the loan of their Gyro rowing machine.
The David Lloyd Centre at Raynes Park for location shots of their gym.

Pete Serjeant for full-color illustrations.
Rob Shone and Paul Wilding for line drawings.
Hilary Bird for the index and Debbie Rhodes for additional help with
the computer page make-up.